Transforming Storytimes into Reading and Writing Lessons

Annie Weissman

PROFESSIONAL GROWTH SERIES®

A Publication of THE BOOK REPORT & LIBRARY TALK

Linworth Publishing, Inc.
Worthington, Ohio

Dedicated to my friend and colleague, Susan Garvin, and to all the students and staff at the old Roosevelt School, Lassen School, Madison Simis School, Granada Primary School, and Sevilla School, all in Phoenix, Arizona.

Cataloging-in-Publication Data

Weissman, Annie, 1948-
    Transforming storytimes into reading and writing lessons / by Annie Weissman.
        p. cm.
    Includes bibliographical references and index.
    ISBN 1-58683-026-0
    1. Elementary school libraries--Activity programs--United States. 2. Language arts
(Elementary)--United States. 3. Children's literature--Study and teaching
(Elementary)--United States. I. Title.

Z675.S3 W446 2001
027.8'222--dc21

2001038042

Published by Linworth Publishing, Inc.
480 East Wilson Bridge Road, Suite L
Worthington, Ohio 43085

ISBN 1-58683-026-0

5 4 3 2 1

Table of Contents

Table of Contents continued

TRANSFORMING STORYTIMES INTO READING AND WRITING LESSONS

Introduction

Change is necessary for survival, but change is scary. The enthusiastic sharing of books and stories with students may have been sufficient in the past. Now, however, more is required. But with just a few "tweaks," storytime can become an integral part of the curriculum of the school. Therefore, this book's purpose is to assist school library media specialists in incorporating specific learning objectives into a storytime format, thus extending the storytime experience into standards-based reading and writing lessons. The book is intended for veteran and beginning school library media specialists and teachers who collaborate with them. Relevant objectives have been taken from national standards. Objectives from standardized tests are also included. The book has specific plans that are easy to implement. Lists of appropriate books follow each lesson.

One can always find the time if something is deemed important. In these days of standardized testing and accountability, using storytimes in more meaningful ways is an important focus for the school library media specialist. The ideas presented here encourage a common vocabulary so people can communicate about books and stories, and include strategies I have found to be successful for student learning. I hope readers of this work will find the materials useful in transforming their own storytimes.

The lessons in this book are designed for grades one through six but can be adapted for middle school students by adding age-appropriate literature, especially short stories. The lessons can be used with storytime for 20 to 60 students. This book will outline strategies for open-ended questioning and ways for all students to have the opportunity and responsibility to respond. It does not require any fancy equipment, although technology is woven into the units. These strategies can be used with all the storytime favorites. It will take little time and no money to transform storytimes into reading and writing lessons. In my opinion, adding the academic component will not take away from the bonding that happens between reader and listener. Rather, it will expand the possibilities for talking about books. The future of school library media specialists depends on their inclusion in the reading and learning process at school.

The definition of storytime that I have developed for this concept is the enthusiastic and effective reading of the best of children's literature to a group of students. If a picture book is used, the book is held so all the students can see the illustrations as the school library media specialist is reading. This requires that the reader be familiar with the text of the book. Traditional storytelling without a book and flannel board storytelling can also be included, but they are not requirements for storytime.

► HOW THE BOOK IS ORGANIZED

Chapter One discusses the strengths of traditional storytime and the advantages of using storytime for instruction, using objectives from national, state, and local curricula as the basis for lesson planning. Nationally standardized test objectives are also addressed. Examples of specific objectives and books to match those objectives are provided. In Chapter Two, storytimes as reading and writing lessons are related to the implementation of the American Association of School Librarian's (AASL) information literacy standards. The information literacy standards that can be met by storytime are cited and examples given.

> The future of school library media specialists depends on their inclusion in the reading and learning process at school.

The types of lesson plans used in this book are explained in Chapter Three. Particular attention is paid to forming and targeting objectives—the focus of every lesson. Chapter Four presents strategies that allow all students to participate in storytime when it is a reading lesson. These strategies include pair share, Big Books, readers' theater, puppet shows, student flannel board presentations, and choral responses.

In Chapter Five, strategies are explained that allow all students to participate in storytimes when they are writing lessons. The parts of the writing process these strategies address are brainstorming, composing, and publishing. This chapter provides detailed descriptions of the materials needed, with examples of lessons such as composing big and little books with all grades, writing innovations of books read in storytime, writing paragraphs on literary elements, writing creatively based on the study of genre, and information gathering on a country.

The literary elements of character, setting, plot, point of view, and theme are introduced in Chapter Six. For each element there is a teaching definition, sample lessons, and bibliographies of books to support the concepts. Chapter Seven demonstrates how to apply the objectives of compare and contrast and literary elements to the study of the Caldecott Medal books, perennial favorites for storytime. It includes ideas for collaboration with regular classroom, special education, and special area teachers. Also included are sample lessons on literary elements, compare and contrast, and gathering information from the Internet. Scripts of a folk song and two folktales, reflecting Caldecott Medal books, are included to be used as readers' theater, puppet shows, or plays.

A folktale unit is used as a vehicle in Chapter Eight to show how to collaborate with teachers using objectives from national standards cited in Chapter Two. Collaboration should be at the center of storytime. The elements of folklore are described and lessons provided for students to apply these elements to the stories read to them. Two favorite folktales and their flannel board patterns are included. Chapter Nine shows how to use genre books in storytime to teach both reading and writing objectives. Collaboration with the classroom teacher is essential for this unit. Genres included are mystery, fantasy, science fiction, historical fiction, and contemporary realism. Ways to integrate poetry into storytime lessons are described in Chapter Ten.

Teaching students to evaluate nonfiction, one of the information literacy standards included in AASL's *Information Power,* is covered in Chapter Eleven. The chapter also describes teaching students to distinguish between fiction and nonfiction. The Conclusion lists the positive effects of implementing these suggested changes in storytime. A professional bibliography is included at the end of the book.

⊃ MY EXPERIENCE

As a career educator, I've been working with students and literature for more than 30 years. My experience includes preschool through graduate school. In the late seventies, while serving as an elementary school librarian, I was asked to teach an "extra" period of reading for gifted students in grades five and six. I used strategies and concepts from the Great Books program and the whole language approach to reading, as well as Rebecca Lukens' *A Critical Handbook of Children's Literature* (HarperCollins, 1999), which was used as a textbook in a course I taught for Arizona State University. I felt strongly that these academically talented students, mostly from ethnic minorities, needed to be able to clearly articulate ideas about literature so any teacher would immediately label them as "smart" and have high expectations of them. The students did well and enjoyed the class, according to their grades and evaluations of the course.

> I felt strongly that these academically talented students, mostly from ethnic minorities, needed to be able to clearly articulate ideas about literature so any teacher would immediately label them as "smart" and have high expectations of them.

I moved to a model bilingual school and was asked to provide a similar program for third and fourth graders as well as for fifth and sixth graders. I refined some concepts and added a framework from Glenna Davis Sloan's *The Child as Critic* (Teachers College Press, 1991), which I'd used as a text to teach a graduate library science class at Arizona State University. The elementary school students grasped the concepts, and then I started to expand the ideas to picture books in my regular storytimes for grades one, two, and three. I was surprised that almost all of the students who were not in the gifted programs also were able to understand and apply the concepts. However, I was dissatisfied with the questioning techniques for large groups. While working on my administrative certificate, I took several graduate courses in instruction and instructional supervision that included cooperative learning techniques and active participation strategies.

I left the school library and became an assistant principal. Part of my job was to implement the Big Book and writing programs in the primary grades. I selected and used strategies from many trainers. As a school administrator, I observed both best teaching practices and some teaching that was not exemplary. When I became a principal at another school two years later, I assisted the teachers in implementing these high quality programs and strategies. When I returned to the school library, after an absence of seven years, I brought these ideas with me and incorporated them into storytime in order to make it an essential part of the school curriculum.

To give the reader a context in which to better understand the perspective presented in this book, I work in an urban elementary school with 1,600 students from preschool to sixth grade. The students come from diverse cultural and linguistic backgrounds. Seventy-nine percent of the students qualify for free or reduced lunch. My staff includes two part-time clerical assistants. The library media center, along with the rest of the special areas, runs on a six- rather than five-day schedule. Each student in preschool to second grade participates in a 20-minute storytime every six days. The periods overlap. For example, one first grade class comes in for 10 minutes to check out, then sits in the story dome. Another first grade class joins them, and both classes have a 20-minute storytime. Then the first class leaves and the second class has 10 minutes to check out books. This is not the optimal experience, but is done to accommodate the number of students at the school. Storytime would be more effective with one class at a time. The students in grades three through six have a more flexible schedule.

The program outlined in this book can be implemented immediately. Only the desire to do so is needed. Start with the section that is most comfortable and move toward the more challenging. Change is not only necessary, but it can also be rewarding and painless. I invite the reader to begin the process of modifying and expanding storytimes so they can be more meaningful experiences for children, using the lessons and strategies presented in this book.

CHAPTER 1

Do Traditional Storytimes Meet the Needs of Today's Children?

School library media specialists, children's librarians, teachers, parents, and grandparents are urged to read to children. Jim Trelease writes in *The Read Aloud Handbook* (Penguin, 1995) that extensive research has proven that reading aloud to a child is the single most important factor in raising a reader (3). Trelease asserts that reading aloud conditions children to associate reading with pleasure (8). It creates background knowledge, which is important for vocabulary development, increases understanding of subjects, and compares new information with stored knowledge (11-12). In *The Power of Reading* (Libraries Unlimited, 1993), Stephen Krashen also cites important information gained from research. Specifically, the research cited on page 39 shows that when teachers read and discuss books with students, students read more.

The strengths of storytime in the library, classroom, and home are many. Reading aloud develops children's interests, and widens and varies their experiences. It acquaints children with the formal language of books and broadens their vocabulary. A word is more easily decoded if the reader has an oral familiarity with it. Ruth Sawyer, in *The Way of the Storyteller* (Viking, 1942, 1962), says that through the selection of titles, storytime can develop children's senses of curiosity and humor (167), and widen their reading interests (177). Reading aloud allows children to enjoy books that they can understand but are too difficult for them to read independently.

Reading aloud also breaks down the barrier of the "harder" books. If the books are carefully chosen, they can give children a taste for good literature as well as introduce them to different genres. The choices for storytime can be related directly to curricular content. Reading aloud creates the model of the adult as a reader and extends warmth and the human bonds to books and reading.

After 28 years of observation, I can say that storytime is an enjoyable way to increase a child's attention span. Four-year-old students in Headstart and transitional kindergarten can listen to a story for 10 minutes or less at the beginning of the school year. By January, these students are listening to stories attentively for 20 minutes. The same is true of the special education students who have learning or emotional handicaps. Perhaps most significant gains can be observed in those students labeled "moderately retarded." In classrooms and libraries, reading aloud should be done regularly—not as a reward, but daily.

▷ THE TRADITIONAL VS. CONTEMPORARY PHILOSOPHY OF STORYTIME

Marie Shedlock, in her classic *The Art of the Storyteller* (Dover, 1951), originally published in 1915, represents the traditional view of storytime. According to Shedlock, storytime should weave an unbroken spell. After the story is told, students should not be asked to answer questions, or to reproduce or illustrate the story (127). Instead Shedlock suggests five minutes of silence after the story (150).

> Too often a question is posed, and one child answers. The other students are free to tune out, or worse yet, to think that their answers do not matter.

I agreed with Shedlock for years. Talking about books with children is fraught with problems. One pitfall is the "test trap." Children should not feel stressed to provide the "right" answer. Another problem is ensuring that all children share their ideas in a realistic time frame. Too often a question is posed, and one child answers. The other students are free to tune out, or worse yet, to think that their answers do not matter. Often the questions asked after a story are literal and do not require higher level thinking skills. Jamie McKenzie, in *Beyond Technology: Questioning, Research and the Information Literate School* (FNO Press, 2000), discusses the types of questions to ask and how to frame them (26–32). The following is a sample of the types of questions:

■ Strategic (What thinking tool is the most likely to work?)
■ Elaborating (What is the implied meaning?)
■ Inventive (How can the information be grouped and regrouped so it means more?)
■ Divergent (What further ideas do I have, based on the information given?)

▷ CURRENT RESEARCH

Research cited in "Dick and Jane Go to the Head of the Class," an article by Christine Hamilton-Pennell, Keith Curry Lance, Narcia Rodney, and Eugene Hainer in the April 1, 2000 issue of *School Library Journal*, demonstrates the benefits of a professional library media specialist who collaborates with teachers, teaches information literacy skills, and serves as an instructional leader. In a parallel study in Alaska, conducted by Lance, a higher percentage of students in schools with library media specialists scored proficient or above on state reading tests when compared to students in schools *without* a developed library media program. In Lance's Pennsylvania study, test scores increased in schools where professional librarians spent time on instructional activities. Finally, Lance's study in his home state of Colorado showed student scores increased when library media specialists were part of the instructional leadership. More information can be found at Library Research Service's Web site at <www.lrs.org>.

▶ NCTE/IRA STANDARDS

Storytime can be so much more without taking away the positive aspects of the traditional reading aloud. Students are required to learn more these days. There are state standards and local standards, with accompanying assessments, as well as national standards set by the National Council of Teachers of English (NCTE) and the International Reading Association (IRA). Nationally standardized tests, such as the Iowa Test of Basic Skills and the Stanford 9, are viewed by the public as proof of how well their school and children are doing. These standards and tests can be addressed in storytime.

The NCTE/IRA standards, available at <www.ncte.org/standards>, speak directly to storytime. The standards can and should be met in other ways, but why waste the opportunity to use quality children's literature? Standards One and Two require students to read a wide range of print and literature, including many genres. Careful selection of books to read aloud allows students to experience historical fiction, science fiction, fantasy, mysteries, contemporary realism, fables, folktales, and poetry. For example, understanding the structure of a mystery story can add to students' grasp of the concept of a story's beginning, middle, and end, for reading and for writing. Chapter Eleven covers specific lessons and genre selections.

NCTE/IRA Standard Three requires students to apply a variety of strategies to comprehend, interpret, evaluate, and appreciate books. When reading aloud a quality children's book, such as *Swimmy* by Leo Lionni (Pantheon, 1963), you can students about themes. Information on literary elements and how to apply them are included in Chapter Seven.

> **A higher percentage of students in schools with library media specialists scored proficient or above on state reading tests when compared to students in schools without a developed library media program.**

NCTE/IRA Standard Four requires students to communicate orally and effectively with a variety of audiences. The scripts in Chapters Six and Eight, using the content of Caldecott books and folktales, can be used to meet this standard as can the flannel board stories included in Chapter Eight. The book, upon which a script is based, is read at storytime to familiarize students with the characters, plot, and vocabulary. The students can use the scripts to present readers' theater, puppet shows, or plays for other students or their parents.

NCTE/IRA Standard Six specifies that students apply their knowledge of genre to create, evaluate, and discuss books. Chapter Ten on genre shows how to use storytime to teach students how to talk and write in various genres. Using the active participation strategies in Chapter Four, teachers and librarians can ensure that all students learn these skills.

NCTE/IRA Standard Seven requires that students do information gathering to be able to evaluate facts. These skills will be addressed in Chapter Eight in a lesson where students gather facts about different countries and compare those facts. The lessons in the nonfiction chapter focus on evaluating the scope and accuracy of information when facts from two books on the same subject are compared.

▶ STATE AND LOCAL STANDARDS

Minnesota and Arizona have good examples of state standards that are clear and concise. The Minnesota Department of Children, Families & Learning Standards, available at <www.mecr/state.mn.us>, require that both primary and intermediate grade students interpret and evaluate fiction and nonfiction in order to understand implicit ideas, make predictions, draw conclusions, compare and contrast elements of the story, and distinguish fact from fiction. Students must identify the main ideas with supporting details. These objectives are perfect for storytime. Two books can be carefully chosen for storytime so the elements in these stories can be compared and contrasted.

The Arizona Department of Education, at <www.ade.state.az.us/standards/language-arts/>, has similar objectives. They are more detailed, but contain similar threads. For assessment, students in grades one through three need to draw conclusions, summarize, make predictions, identify cause and effect, differentiate between fiction and nonfiction, define and differentiate characters, compare characters, plots, and settings, and describe the literary elements of fiction and nonfiction. The objectives for grades four through eight are the same but more in-depth. All of these objectives can be taught in storytime by prefacing the reading with a short lesson on what to look and listen for in the book. The lessons in Chapter Six are examples of this.

The Arizona writing standards for first through eighth grades require students to write stories that include a sequenced plot, developed characters, and settings. The instructional objectives for grades four through eight require students to write an expository essay that begins with a thesis with an introductory statement, and ends with a paragraph concluding the development of the thesis, a summary, or a clincher idea. The essay must develop ideas with supporting details, facts, examples, or descriptions, and include personal interpretation, analysis, and evaluation to show their understanding of the subject. These are not assessed at this grade level. These objectives will be addressed in Chapter Five on writing strategies, Chapter Six on literary elements, and Chapter Ten on how to use storytime to teach students to write specific aspects of a genre.

> It is essential that school library media specialists have copies of their state and local standards.

It is essential that school library media specialists have copies of their state and local standards. Most of the states publish their standards on the Internet. The curriculum coordinator of the school district has the local standards, which drive the school's curriculum. These standards and their assessments address the why, what, and how of what is taught.

▶ STANDARDIZED TESTS

Each spring most students take a nationally normed test. School library media specialists should share the teaching of many of the objectives for these tests. Although the objectives tested are a fraction of the scope and sequence, they overlap the national, state, and local objectives. In grade two, the questions on the Stanford Achievement Test (SAT 9) address prediction, sequencing, genre, inferences, and word meaning in context. In grades three and four, all of these are tested with the addition of main idea, setting, problem/solution, and compare and contrast. In grade five, main character and details are added. In grade six, theme and the elements of literature are added. This listing tells when these areas are tested. They should be introduced at least one year prior to testing to achieve mastery. Each chapter of this book suggests plans and ways of teaching these objectives through storytimes. The chapter on lesson plans will address how these skills can become objectives for storytimes.

▶ CONCLUSION

These standardized tests and the expectations inherent in standards-based education have raised the educational "bar" for students. However, many of these objectives can be taught with storytime. It takes new strategies as well as all members of the faculty working together. It is not hard to transform the storytime already being offered to include these objectives and make storytime an integral part of the language arts curriculum. However, in order to effect change, the library media specialist or teacher must understand the objectives thoroughly. What are literary elements? How exactly are characters differentiated? How can characters be compared? What are the purposes of a setting? What is genre? How can these concepts be written as performance objectives? How can all students be made responsible for meeting these objectives? All of these questions will be answered in ensuing chapters.

Based on the previously presented information, it becomes apparent that traditional storytimes do not meet the needs of today's students, though some aspects of the "transformed storytime" have the same elements as the traditional ones. The selection of titles for storytime should still be taken from the best in children's literature. The reader's enthusiasm and oral interpretation remains the same. However, storytime must be part of the language arts program of the school, with the library media specialist as a leader. Transformed storytimes have specific objectives. All students are expected to actively participate as well as learn the good listening skills that traditional storytime fosters.

CHAPTER 2

Storytime and the Implementation of *Information Power*

The American Association of School Librarians (AASL) published *Information Power: Building Partnerships for Learning* (American Library Association, 1998) as a refinement of the standards set in *Information Power: Guidelines for Library Media Programs* (American Library Association, 1988). The new standards are commonly referred to as *IP 2.* These standards revolve around three interwoven duties of the school library media specialist: learning and teaching, program administration, and information access and delivery. The curriculum, the information literacy standards for students' learning, is contained in a circle of leadership, collaboration, and technology. At first these standards may seem overwhelming at the elementary level, but as one rereads and reflects, it becomes clear that with a change to storytime, many of the standards can be met. Flexibility is the key.

This chapter will address Standards Five and Seven, as will Chapter Three, "Collaboration, Leadership, and Technology," and Chapter Four, "Teaching and Learning."

▷ INFORMATION LITERACY STANDARD FIVE

Standard Five, on pages 26–29, states that independent learners are information literate and appreciate literature. Indicator 1, that the student is a successful and self–motivated reader, has three levels. On the *basic* level, students can explain and discuss fiction. To be *proficient*, students can analyze plots, themes, and characters. This is similar to the NCTE/IRA Standards One, Two, and Three:

■ Students read a wide range of print and nonprint texts to build an understanding of texts, of themselves, and of cultures of the United States and the world; to acquire new information; to respond to the needs and demands of society and the workplace; and for personal fulfillment . . .

■ Students read a wide range of literature from many periods in many genres to build an understanding of the many dimension (e.g., philosophical, ethical, aesthetic) of human experience.

■ Students apply a wide range of strategies to comprehend, interpret, evaluate, and appreciate texts . . .

Both of these levels are relevant to elementary school and can be taught through story-time. Starting in grade one, students can be taught a common language to talk about books. This "language" of literary elements is covered in Chapter Six. Storytime can also provide a wide range of listening experiences. So much can be accomplished with a short lesson before the story is read and a few effective questions afterward. Indicator 2 of Standard Five of *IP 2* is that students compose creative products in a variety of formats. The *basic* level requires a simple format. The *proficient* level requires the combination of several formats. The *basic* level can be achieved via readers' theater, puppet shows, flannel board stories, retelling and innovations of picture books, travel brochures, and graphs. The extent to which the *proficient* level can be addressed depends on the technology and staffing of the library media center. Both levels require a collaborative relationship with teachers so the products can be created in the library media center and in the classroom. Creative and expository writing products can be based on book discussions.

> So much can be accomplished with a short lesson before the story is read and a few effective questions afterward.

For instance, as students understand each literary element, they can write concise paragraphs applying their knowledge to both picture books and novels. Grades one, two, and three can do this as a group. Students in grades four, five, and six should be able to write their own paragraphs following extensive modeling by the school library media specialist and the teacher. The graphic organizer near the end of Chapter Seven represents the culmination of this activity, an oral or written discussion of all the elements as seen in one book. Students can also create characters, descriptions of settings, and plot problems. They can introduce themes into their own stories and play with a point of view.

First grade classes, after listening to a story filled with rhymed text, can create an innovation of that text as a group. That new text can be typed on a word processor and copied so each student can illustrate the book and use it to learn to read. This book can be taken home and shared over and over with members of the student's family. A large print version of the same story can be made into either a bulletin board or a Big Book with illustrations from each student.

▶ INFORMATION LITERACY STANDARD SEVEN

IP 2's Standard Seven addresses information gathering. The *basic* level requires that students identify several appropriate sources for resolving information problems or questions. These information needs can arise from storytime if open-ended questions are posed from fiction and nonfiction selections read aloud.

For example, when reading Caldecott books, students are curious about the medal and the person. Who gives it? How often? When was it first given? Who is Randolph Caldecott? When did he live? What do his illustrations look like? Did Randolph Caldecott win the medal named for him? These questions can be answered by a variety of sources: general encyclopedias, specialized encyclopedias, books on awards, and the online catalog (to locate books illustrated by Randolph Caldecott).

When reading folktales aloud, students notice the subtleties of the illustrations that show geography, weather, clothing, food, and customs of different cultures. These can be researched to compare and contrast with life in their community.

▷ COLLABORATION

Chapter Three of *IP 2* lays out the three intertwined circles of the school library media specialist's job. Most veteran school library media specialists are involved with program administration. They are comfortable with the duties of selecting, purchasing, processing, and circulating materials. All provide some instruction in meeting informational needs and access to materials. A few changes in storytime can make the school library media specialist integral to the learning process.

To accomplish the goals of *IP 2's* fourth chapter, "Teaching and Learning," the library media specialist must become an expert on curriculum goals: those of the school district, the state, and the objectives of standardized tests, as well as the state and district assessments of students. Knowledge is power. Awareness of the objectives allows the library media specialist to plan lessons to incorporate them into storytime.

Collaborative relationships can be built a few at a time. There is always an accommodating, friendly, teacher at lunch. Discuss specific objectives. Decide which objectives to collaborate on first. Teachers will be impressed that someone else is going to share the burden of instruction. Use lunchtime conversation to plan your storytimes for specific literary elements or thinking skills. Make sure to inform the teacher what you have planned and provide the teacher with picture books that reinforce each objective. Start small and build gradually. Once one second grade class has been introduced to the objectives and mastered their application, the teacher will see the difference in his or her own classroom. The news will spread like ants on icing. Another second grade teacher will ask for the same instruction. Lesley J. Farmer, in *Workshops for Teachers: Becoming Partners for Information Literacy* (9), suggests that products of team planning, like bibliographies, be posted on teacher bulletin boards or put in teachers' mailboxes. A project can be shared at a faculty meeting or reported in a newsletter. The principal can be informed by casual conversations or in monthly reports. It is effective to display the students' writings and illustrations on a bulletin board located in a main hallway of the school.

> Use lunchtime conversation to plan your storytimes for specific literary elements or thinking skills.

Another way to initiate collaboration is to attend grade-level meetings and offer to plan with teachers for a specific required skill or project. Once the project is decided upon, meet with the teacher(s) to write out the plan of action, including who will be responsible for each part of the lessons. For further information on collaborative planning, consult Donna P. Miller and J'Lynn Anderson's *Developing an Integrated Library Program* (Linworth, 1996).

There are always some teachers who eagerly use the library media center and request services. These teachers are prime candidates for collaboration. When one asks about materials for a colonial unit, suggest that you plan activities that will meld the library and classroom while addressing specific objectives from curriculum standards.

Do not expect involvement from all the teachers. There are always a few holdouts, at least for the first year or two. Do not waste your time and energy on them, but do as much for their students on your own as you can. See David V. Loertscher's *Taxonomies of the School Library Media Program* (Hi Willow, 2000) for more ideas.

▶ TEACHING AND LEARNING

Problem solving and thinking skills directly correlate to changes in the types of questions asked at the ends of stories. Students engage in higher order thinking skills when they are asked to arrive at conclusions that produce new meaning or understanding for them. Chapter Three will discuss in more detail Bloom's taxonomy of educational objectives, which explains the hierarchical nature of thinking skills. When students learn the elements of folktales, it is on the knowledge level of thinking skills. However, when they apply these elements and are able to use specific examples from specific folktales, they are at a higher level—application. If they write stories in the folktale style using the elements, they are at the highest level of thinking—synthesis.

When students compare and contrast books presented at storytime, they are using higher level thinking skills. When they critique books based on stated standards, they are evaluating, a very high level of thinking. Similarly, when students compare the information in two nonfiction books with the same content, they are thinking at a higher level. When they evaluate the bias, point of view, and accuracy, they are again at the highest level of thinking.

The five principles in Chapter Four of *IP 2* require the school library media specialist to collaborate with teachers. For principles one and two, school library media programs must become part of the learning and teaching program of the school. Making storytime reading and writing lessons with curricular objectives can accomplish this.

> Students engage in higher order thinking skills when they are asked to arrive at conclusions that produce new meaning or understanding for them.

To accomplish Principle Three, the library media specialist must model and promote collaborative planning and curriculum development. For example, when planning storytime for kindergarten, it is important to find out on which objectives the teacher is focusing. If the language arts curriculum is an alphabetical letter a week, secure a list of the letters to be taught each week. Make sure all books in storytime relate to the letter taught each week. Start the storytime with "Which letter are you studying this week?" Expect a choral response. The next question is "What sound does that letter make?" Gather books and media that relate to that letter and deliver them to the teachers. If the kindergarten uses the integrated approach, with the objectives grouped by units, get a list of the units for the month. Make sure your storytime is fiction or nonfiction books about the unit. This is good old-fashioned library service.

If some teachers are not currently interested in collaborating, go with the ones who are. If possible, try to involve more than one teacher. If you can collaborate with all the fourth grade teachers on the objectives, it is easier to manage the planning process. Try including other special area teachers. For example, for a Caldecott unit, invite the art and music teachers to your planning sessions. The art teacher may be willing to plan lessons investigating the techniques used by Caldecott illustrators. The music teacher may be willing to teach the students songs related to Caldecott books. For the folktale unit, ask the music teacher to introduce the students to folk songs and instruments from the various countries from which certain folktales originate.

Principle Four is about the library media specialist using and promoting creative, effective, and collaborative teaching. This can be accomplished by using the strategies discussed in Chapters Four and Five of this book.

Principle Six, encouraging students to read and listen for understanding and enjoyment, is the epitome of transformed storytimes. Most library media programs already measure enjoyment of books by the way the stories are read aloud, with expression and enthusiasm. The addition of reading and writing lessons incorporates the component of understanding. For example, before reading *Train to Somewhere* by Eve Bunting (Clarion, 1996) to fourth grade students, the library media specialist can either explain historical fiction and how it can be evaluated or explain the functions of setting in a story. After the book is read, students reflect on either of these issues and share their thoughts with a partner. Before reading *Finders Keepers* by Will and Nichols (Harcourt Brace, 1951) to second graders, the library media specialist can preface it with a short explanation of theme. Afterwards, students reflect and share what the themes of the book are and how these themes relate to their own lives.

Principle Eight requires the library media program to support the learning of all students, including those with differing abilities, styles, and needs. Transformed storytimes allow students of widely different achievement and ability levels to understand new concepts and apply them. Most children's listening comprehension is much higher than their independent reading comprehension. It also allows those students who cannot read to participate fully in the learning process.

Special education students can experience success in the storytime setting. Although a child may not be able to read, the child can come up with a rhyme, whether it is original or remembered from context, after hearing three rhymed books and singing a rhymed song.

▶ CONCLUSION

In conclusion, if storytime is carefully planned around learning objectives that are the product of collaboration with classroom teachers, and effective teaching strategies are employed, the school library media specialist becomes a strong educational force within the school.

CHAPTER 3

Changing Storytime Lesson Plans to Make Them Reading and Writing Lessons

The lesson plans in this book do not include all the elements of good lessons, but they *do* show how to make lessons active and link storytime to reading and writing objectives, which is the purpose of this book. They are written in the style of Madeline Hunter's *Mastery Teaching* (Corwin Press, 1982). The *review* section of each lesson links students' experiences or prior lessons to the current lesson. The *objectives* are all based on local, state, or national standards, or standardized test skills and objectives. This emphasizes the library media specialist as essential to the learning process. The objectives are performance based, meaning they are written so students must do something. The *direct whole group instruction* includes short concept teaching and the reading of trade books. The *student practice* includes active participation strategies, detailed in Chapters Four and Five, to ensure that all the students are thinking and responding. It is synonymous with Hunter's *guided practice*. During this phase the library media specialist observes, listens, and evaluates whether the students are accomplishing the lesson objective. The *closure* is to reinforce the students' learning. It is best to have active participation in this phase.

⮞ OBJECTIVES

All lesson planning should start with the objective being taught. Lesson plans for traditional story times usually have objectives such as the following:

- Students will learn to listen attentively to the story being read.

- Students will become familiar with the best in children's literature on the topic of ___ (food, farm animals, dogs, weather, a specific holiday).

These are passive objectives for students and are not measurable. By changing the objectives so students are required to be active, a step is made toward performance assessment. The specific objective states what the students are to know and to be able to do as a result of the lesson. The objective guides the school library media specialist in selecting learning activities, tells the students what is expected, and gives a standard for evaluating progress. For more information on writing objectives, consult *How to Write and Use Instructional Objectives* by Norman E. Gronlund (Merrill, 2000).

The objectives should be chosen from the district and state curricula, as well as those that reflect national language arts standards, *IP 2*, and objectives of nationally normed tests. Sample objectives are the following:

- Students will compare and contrast the setting of the two books to which they have listened.

> By changing the objectives so students are required to be active, a step is made toward performance assessment.

- Students will identify the main character, and make inferences about what he is like by what he says, does, looks like, what others say about him, and what the author says about him.

- Students will discern the difference between the fiction and non-fiction books they've listened to, and identify facts that were woven into the fiction book.

- Students will evaluate whether a story to which they've listened meets the criteria of a specific genre.

- Students will write a paragraph about the conflict in a specific picture book.

- Students will compose new verses for the song "A Hunting We Will Go."

- Students will brainstorm several reminiscences of a favorite relative.

All of these objectives require the student to be an active participant. All of these objectives are based on local, state, national, or test objectives.

Any discussions of objectives should include the ideas of B. S. Bloom's Taxonomy of Educational Objectives. A summary of cognitive objectives is included on pages 111–112 in Appendix B of *How to Write and Use Instructional Objectives* by Norman E. Gronlund, (Merrill, 2000). The skills are hierarchical from understanding (remembering things learned), to comprehension (getting the meaning of what was learned), to application (using the learning in new situations), to analysis (breaking something down to smaller parts in order to understand its organization), to synthesis (putting together ideas in a new way), to evaluation (judging the value of something for a specific purpose).

An example of an understanding objective is that the student will recall that the plot of a story usually has a conflict. Students who demonstrate comprehension should be able to state the information in their own words. For example, the comprehension objective would be accomplished if the student said that the plot of a story usually has a problem in it. For an objective on the application level, the student has to be able to use the concept. If *Caps for Sale* by Esphyr Slobodkina (Scott, 1940) was read, the student would be able to state that there was a problem or conflict between the peddler and the monkeys. At the analysis level, the objective would be for students to figure out the type of conflict in the book. There are several good answers: person against person, the peddler against the monkeys who stole his caps, person against society because the monkeys broke a societal rule by stealing, and person against society because the peddler is hungry and not able to make money for food since no one bought his hats.

At the synthesis level, the students combine elements to make a new, unique product. An objective written at this level, using the book *Caps for Sale*, would be to have the students think of different ways for the peddler to get his caps back from the monkeys.

At the evaluation level, students decide whether a given product meets specified criteria, or students compare two products for a purpose and back up their answers. To complete an objective at this level, students should be able to compare the monkeys' behavior in *Caps for Sale* with the monkey's behavior in *The Crocodile and the Monkey* by Paul Galdone (Houghton Mifflin, 1969) and answer which acted more like a person and why.

Once the objective has been chosen, it is necessary to link that objective to students' experiences or learning. If the objective is in an area new to the students, plan a practical way to link it to the students' experience. For instance, if the objective is for students to identify the setting of a book, first review the setting of the storytime (in the library, in a school, in the city, in the state, in the U.S., in the morning or afternoon, in the year 2001).

▶ LINKING STORIES WITH OBJECTIVES

Most veteran library media specialists and teachers are familiar with reading stories as the direct whole group instruction. But it is necessary to link the stories being read to the objective. This usually involves a short, two- or three-sentence explanation of the objective. For example, if the objective is for students to identify the setting of a book, then it is necessary to define setting as the time and place of a book. Long-winded explanations are not necessary. All that is needed is one sentence and a link to the review that the time of the storytime is the present year, in the morning or afternoon, and that the place is school, in local city, in the state, in the United States. Then one story is read. If the concept is totally new, then part of the direct instruction is for the school library media specialist to model the objective before asking the students to do so. If this is the case, then after the objective is modeled, another story is read.

> Once the objective has been chosen, it is necessary to link that objective to students' experiences or learning. If the objective is in an area new to the students, plan a practical way to link it to the students' experience.

▶ GUIDED PRACTICE AND CLOSURE

The *guided student practice* is done by using the active participation strategies provided in Chapters Four and Five. If pair share is used, it must be monitored closely by the library media specialist and the classroom teacher by listening to the quality of the students' conversations, ensuring that all students are participating, and evaluating whether the students were able to perform the objective.

Closure wraps up the lesson, reminding the students of what they've learned. Merely having students reiterate answers is not enough. This must be done in conjunction with the library media specialist's summary of the question and why the answers were appropriate. For example, for *Train to Somewhere* by Eve Bunting (Clarion, 1996), the library media specialist asks the students to chorally respond to where the story took place. The students respond, "On a train going west." She then asks the students to chorally respond to "When did the story take place?" The students respond "1878." Then the library media specialist says, "Yes, the setting of the story is the time and place of the story."

CHAPTER 4

Active Participation Strategies for Storytime Reading Lessons

▶ GETTING STUDENTS' ATTENTION

It is essential that all children be invited and required to participate in learning. The first thing that must be done is to literally get their attention. Procedures must be taught so transitions from one activity to another go smoothly. The signal for quiet can be a raised hand or a short series of claps repeated by the students. The latter gets some of the students' attention, and their claps alert the rest of the class that it is time to be quiet and pay attention. This procedure needs to be used after each partner activity to signal that it is time to listen.

▶ PAIR SHARE

"Pair share" is an active participation strategy that can be used in a multitude of settings and lessons. It is particularly effective for questions after a story is read. The purpose of pair share is to make all students responsible for thinking and to allow all students to respond. The school library media specialist should have high expectations of all students. By actively monitoring the pairs, the school library media specialist can evaluate the effectiveness of a lesson.

Jamie McKenzie, in his book *Beyond Technology: Questioning, Research and the Information Literate School* (6), states that:

> Questions are intended to provoke thought and inspire reflection, but all too often the process is short circuited by the simple answer, the quick truth or the appealing placebo.

In order for active participation in storytime to be worthwhile, the questions have to be worth thinking about and answering. McKenzie presents many ideas for questioning strategies, including a chapter on "Provoking Fresh Thought and Deep Reasoning with Dissonance, Contrast and Juxtaposition." By presenting students with two books that are different and juxtaposing them, dissonance is created. People are uncomfortable with dissonance. They search to find similarities and differences to resolve the dissonance, leading to resonance and to insight. The compare and contrast lessons in this book, as well as the following lesson, contain such an example.

When a question is posed after a story, there must be "think time." Students may not talk or raise their hands during this time, allowing everyone to think of an answer to the question. Allow 30 seconds to three minutes of think time, depending on the complexity of the question. This time is necessary, because the questions asked will not be on the simple recall level. After the think time, pair the students where they are seated. Extend your hand to signal which students are paired. If you simply say, "Tell the person next to you," several minutes or more will be lost as the students figure out their partners.

Give the partners enough time for one to share before saying, "Make sure both partners share." Monitor to make sure that all the pairs are sharing. If the sharing is not monitored, students quickly learn that the person in charge is not serious about each student being responsible for thinking.

> Too often a question is posed, and one child answers. The other students are free to tune out, or worse yet, to think that their answers do not matter.

Be specific in directions. If a comparison is expected, say, "Think of two things that are different about these two books and two things that are the same." This requires students to go beyond their "off the top of the head" answer and to delve deeper. After the pairs share, use the signal to quiet them. It is not necessary to call on the students who have their hands up. In fact, it is better not to allow students to raise their hands. This helps to ensure that all students are engaged. All of the students have answers. Make sure to ask many opinions. There are many right answers, but there are some wrong answers that cannot be supported by the text or pictures.

For example, after listening to *Where the Wild Things Are* by Maurice Sendak (Harper, 1963) and *The Funny Little Woman* by Arlene Mosel (Dutton, 1972), the students are asked to compare the books by thinking of at least two things that are the same and two things that are different. After think time, the students are paired and given two or three minutes to discuss their ideas. The school library media specialist claps her hands three times to signal attention. When everyone is quiet, she elicits responses from students. Sample responses might be the following:

SIMILARITIES:
- They both go to a strange place.
- Both books have some pictures with no words.
- There were monsters in both books.
- Neither the little woman nor Max was afraid of the monsters.
- Both the little woman and Max decided when they would leave and made their own way home.
- They both won the Caldecott Medal.
- Water was the way in and out of both strange places.

■ They both got something good when they got home. Max found his supper and his home. The little woman got rich.

DIFFERENCES:

■ Although both main characters were human, one was a little boy and the other was a woman.

■ Max had been naughty. The little woman was good.

■ Max came home empty-handed from the strange place. The little woman took the magic paddle.

■ Max was in charge of the Wild Things, but the Oni were in charge of the little woman.

Sometimes wrong answers can be turned into correct responses. If a student says, "Max had a good time, but the little woman didn't," go back to the text of *The Funny Little Woman* and read what she says when she tries the magic paddle. "What fun I shall have, making rice dumplings." Then say to the student, "Was the little woman happy about using the magic paddle?" After the student agrees, then say, "So, a similarity is that both Max and the little woman enjoyed their time in the strange land." After the students share their answers, repeat the answers to emphasize their worth.

The same technique can be used when modeling a response. For example, when teaching setting, use pair share to establish the time and place of the book. The school library media specialist can take that further by suggesting the purpose of the setting. During the next lesson, the students can be reminded of the purpose of the setting of the book read during the previous lesson, and asked what the purpose of the setting is in the book for the current lesson.

> ## COOPERATIVE GROUPS

In storytime groups of 15 to 25 students, the library media specialist can employ additional active participation strategies. The school library media specialist forms small groups of four to five students. Each group is given a copy of the story read. One student is the recorder. The students are given a question and asked to come up with as many responses as possible. This technique encourages brainstorming. The question is reiterated and the students then evaluate their responses to see if they answered the question correctly using specifics from the story read.

> ## CHORAL RESPONSE AND CHORAL READING

Choral response, all students answering at the same time, is a traditional but appropriate and effective active participation strategy, especially for literal questions. Students still need think time. This technique allows each student to be responsible for answering the question while the library media specialist makes sure that everyone responds and understands.

Choral reading can be effectively done with "big books" if the print is large and the text minimal. It is best to read the big book alone first. Invite the students to participate during the second reading while the school library media specialist points to the words.

> Choral response, all students answering at the same time, is a traditional but appropriate and effective active participation strategy, especially for literal questions.

▶ PUPPET SHOWS AND READERS' THEATER

There are scripts included in the Caldecott and folktale chapters. These can be used for readers' theater or puppet shows. For readers' theater, the book should be read by the library media specialist before the activity. Divide the group into the number of parts and assign each small group a part. The students in the group chorally read their character's or a narrator's part. Assign the parts so there is a strong reader in each group to model expression and fluency.

For puppet shows, the assigning of the parts is the same. The readers stand in front of the puppet stage, facing the audience, half on one side, half on the other. Choose the puppeteers by having one person in the group use that puppet. If there are to be several performances, allow several students to practice with the puppets. If the script contains repetition and many characters, such as *Frog Went A' Courting, Drummer Hoff,* or *There Was An Old Woman*, all the students can be in front of the audience, and each student can hold a stick puppet and show it at the appropriate time.

▶ FLANNEL BOARD STORYTELLING

Students gain valuable public speaking experience when they present a flannel board story. These stories should be told and modeled several times before the students attempt to tell the stories. Make a cassette tape of the stories so those who are aural learners or nonreaders can learn the stories. The students may either draw their own characters or color the ones provided by the library media specialist. A small amount of felt tape, available in most instructional supply stores, is attached to the back of each character.

> **Students gain valuable public speaking experience when they present a flannel board story.**

Flannel boards are easy to make from cardboard and flannel. This is a great job for a volunteer who wants to work at home. Save the heavy cardboard in book boxes for the boards. Note that uncut boxes do not make good flannel board because the boards need to stand at a slant for the characters to adhere.

Make at least seven or eight boards, although enough for half the class is optimal so that one child is telling and one is listening during the practice sessions. If there are seven or eight flannel boards, put the students in small groups by the story they are practicing. That way, they can practice and hear the same story. When it is time for the performance, arrange the students so that different stories are represented in each group. The audience is a lower grade class, divided into small groups. This allows the storytelling experience to be intimate and not intimidating. Parents of the storytellers are invited to join their child's group.

▶ CONCLUSION

If active participation strategies are used, students learn quickly that the library media specialist expects everyone to participate and has strategies to facilitate this. Each student will feel valued and smart.

CHAPTER 5

Active Participation Strategies for Storytime Writing Lessons

▶ MODELED WRITING

Writing lessons should have active participation. However, writing lessons require more modeling of specific skills. One of the most logical ways to proceed is to base writing on the teaching of literary elements in Chapter Six. As each element is learned, the fodder for an essay is created. The ideas from the previous lessons can be written to teach topic sentence, supporting sentences with details, and translating thoughts into written expression. This activity relates to the NCTE/IRA Standard Three (students must be able to comprehend, interpret, and appreciate books) as well as to NCTE/IRA Standard Six (students should be able to critique and discuss books). After students learn all the literary elements, the skill of weaving all these ideas into an organized and meaningful essay can be taught. This skill can also be taught during "compare and contrast" lessons.

To teach writing by modeling with active participation, you should get writing material from the students. Use pair share from the preceding chapter to elicit responses. For example, have students analyze a character, such as Rotten Ralph in *Rotten Ralph's Rotten Romance* by Jack Gantos (Houghton Mifflin, 1997). As the students respond to the question after pair share, write their ideas on a chart, white board, smart board, or overhead projector. Organize the response page for character under the five categories of looks like, says, does, what others say, and what the author says. The students will have no trouble saying what Ralph is like by what he looks like. Ralph looks like a cat, but he is quite large and red. Students know he is naughty by what he does. He squashes a bug in a valentine, puts ants in the chocolates, shoots arrows at birds, and rubs dog food on his lips. Students discover that Ralph wants others to play fair when he says to himself that Sarah's friend Petunia has cheated at her own game. The students know about Ralph by what others say about him. Sarah says on page 6, "Don't be so difficult." On page 16 she says, "He's very shy." And on page 32 she says, "You are my favorite Valentine." This shows that she loves him, understands him, but is sometimes frustrated by his behavior. The author tells the reader on page 18 "Rotten Ralph did not want to be nice." This lets the reader know that Ralph is not all bad, but he does choose to be rotten at times.

After the students provide ideas for the paragraph, write a cogent paragraph using their ideas. Students should chorally read what the school library media specialist writes. This actively engages students and gives them extra reading practice. If the students are in first or second grade, this can be used as an opportunity to teach them encoding of words. Stop at every third or fourth word, tell the students which word will be written, and ask the group to chorally tell the letters. Choral rereading of the paragraph gives effective closure and provides practice in reading.

In the second modeling session for students in third grade or above, use pair share for them to compose the topic and supporting sentences. The library media specialist writes their ideas for sentences using a smart board, white board, or overhead projector. Have all the students chorally read the completed paragraph on character. Point out to the students how their ideas were used and organized. This modeling should be repeated at least three times before students are asked to write their own paragraphs using the group's ideas. After that is done several times, most students in grades four, five, and six will be ready to write a paragraph on character based on their own ideas.

> After the students provide ideas for the paragraph, write a cogent paragraph using their ideas. Students should chorally read what the school library media specialist writes. This actively engages students and gives them extra reading practice.

The same strategy can be used for compare and contrast. The Caldecott Unit in Chapter Seven gives many examples of how to elicit ideas from students on the comparison of books. The writing segment is an introduction for second graders, a paired activity for third graders, and an independent assignment for fourth graders. Mastery is expected at the fifth or sixth grade level. After pair share, the library media specialist writes the responses on an overhead transparency, chart, white board, or smart board. She then models how to organize, compose, and write a paragraph using the pair share ideas.

The same strategies can be used for all the topics covered in this book: comparison of books, literary elements, elements of folklore, poetry, nonfiction, and genre. First the students' ideas are elicited through pair share. The school library media specialist records the ideas. After the composition of a paragraph is modeled several times, pair share is used to give students practice in composing the topic sentence and the supporting sentences. The students chorally read the completed paragraph. The school library media specialist points out, or has the students point out, the strengths of the paragraph.

▶ SIX TRAITS OF WRITING

Many school districts are using the Six Traits of Writing, developed by the Northwest Regional Educational Laboratory in Portland, Oregon. The six traits they identify are ideas, organization, voice, word choice, sentence fluency, and convention (grammar and spelling.) Each of the six traits can be addressed in storytime. See the Northwest

Regional Laboratory's Web site for suggestions of books for each trait and other information <www.nwel.org>. Pair sharing about a specific trait from a book read aloud provides the details and focus for ideas. The traits of organization and conventions are modeled several times by the library media specialist before guided student practice. Pair share composition provides practice in sentence fluency with the library media specialist modeling and, if necessary, shaping the sentences.

Word choice can be addressed after the rough draft of the paragraph is written as a whole group. The library media specialist selects several words that are not the best choices, or used too often, and asks for suggestions for different words. The use of the thesaurus can be introduced at this time. The voice in these essays is formal. Voice can be taught through the fractured folktales lesson later in this chapter or the point of view lessons in Chapter Six.

▶ GROUP COMPOSITION FOR BIG AND LITTLE BOOKS

Group composition, based on books read at storytime, is another way to involve all students in writing. For example, if *My Little Sister Ate One Hare* by Bill Grossman (Crown, 1996) is read during storytime, the students can compose an innovation based on the rhyme. Using pair share, have the students come up with ideas for numbers one through ten. It's easiest to record these ideas on a sheet of paper. However, a chart, white board, overhead projector, or smart board allows the students to see their ideas. The objective of word choice can be taught by asking students to go beyond the words recorded for a better word or rhyming word.

The school library media specialist takes these ideas and types them using a word processor. At this point choices are made. The new lyrics can be set up so they can be printed out, then copied as a small book for each student to illustrate and take home. In addition, the words can be printed in size 32 or larger, and made into a bulletin board or a big book. To do the latter, the school library media specialist writes what needs to be illustrated, one or two words, on each piece of 8½ x 11 inch paper, ensuring that there are enough pages so each child will draw at least one picture. If the art teacher is collaborating, the illustration can

> Questions for models always arise, giving the school library media specialist impromptu opportunities to show individual students how to use an encyclopedia.

be done during art class. Otherwise the illustrations are drawn instead of having storytime when the class returns to the library. The next time the students come to the school library media center, the pieces of paper are already on the library tables, with colored pencils or crayons at every place. The teacher and the school library media specialist assist first graders and non-readers of any age to read which words they should illustrate. Make sure the students put their names on the papers. Questions for models always arise, giving the school library media specialist impromptu opportunities to show individual students how to use an encyclopedia.

As the students finish their illustrations, the papers are collected. The school library media specialist, or a trained assistant or volunteer, cuts out the illustrations and the students' handwritten names. These are glued (a glue stick is easiest) on sheets of 12 x 18 inch tag board or construction paper with the corresponding words on the page. A title page is printed out and decorated with any extra illustrations. The pages are then laminated and a spiral binder inserted. The big book is read chorally at the next storytime, with careful attention to the name of each illustrator and student's picture. The book is sent back to the classroom with its "authors."

If a bulletin board is desired, the same procedure is used. The pages are not bound, but stapled on the bulletin board in the correct order.

▶ BOOKS THAT LEND THEMSELVES TO INNOVATION

- Brown, Kevin, *The Mucky Pup.* Dutton, 1997. (What other animals could the pup seek out, and how else could he get clean?)
- Cabrera, Jane, *Dog's Day.* Orchard, 2000. (What might a child do with his or her toys?)
- Hillenbrand, Will, *Down by the Station.* Harcourt Brace, 1999. (Where else could the train be headed and what or whom could it pick up?)
- Langstaff, John, *A Hunting We Will Go.* Atheneum, 1974. (For October try *A Haunting We Will Go*)
- Langstaff, John, *Over in the Meadow.* Harcourt Brace, 1985.
- Sandberg, Carl, *The Wedding Procession of the Rag Doll and the Broom Handle and Who Was in It.* Harcourt Brace, 1967. (Who else might be in the wedding procession?)
- Stutson, Caroline, *By the Light of the Halloween Moon.* Lothrop, Lee & Shepard, 1993. (Try By the Light of the —, filling the name of the school, or using the sun, and so on.)
- Tabach, Simms, *I Know an Old Woman Who Swallowed a Fly.* Scholastic, 1997. (What else could she eat besides animals?)
- Van Allsburg, Chris, *The Z Was Zapped.* Houghton Mifflin, 1987. (Students make up their own alphabetic play.)
- Ziefert, Harriet, *The Turnip.* Viking, 1996. (What else could be stuck and who would pull it out?)

▶ CREATIVE WRITING AND STORYTIME FOR THE INTERMEDIATE GRADES

> If the book is to be copied for each student, be careful during the initial brainstorming to screen out ideas that will be too embarrassing, humiliating, or personal for everyone to read.

For students in grades four, five, and six, creative writing can also be a part of storytime. For example, after reading *When I Was Young in the Mountains* by Cynthia Rylant (Dutton, 1982), go back over some of the author's specific reminiscences.

Model a reminiscence of your own along a theme. The theme could be school, a holiday, a vacation, a pet, a grandparent, and so on. Brainstorm three ideas. Choose one of the ideas and develop it, remembering to add sensory details. Organize your paragraph before writing. Create the topic sentence, and so on then the rest of the paragraph with supporting details.

Then it is the students' turn. They brainstorm three ideas and write them down. They follow the same steps as the school library media specialist, ending up with a rough draft. If a final product is desired, the classroom teacher works with the students on revisions and the final copies, using a word processor and leaving a half page each for illustrations. Each student illustrates his or her reminiscence. If the book will be copied for each student, the illustrations should be done in black and white. The pages are collected. The school library media specialist numbers the pages and adds a cover and a title page illustrated by the students. The book is then copied for each student. If the book is to be copied for each student, be careful during the initial brainstorming to screen out ideas that will be too embarrassing, humiliating, or personal for everyone to read. Final products are not required for every writing activity.

One way to integrate writing into the folktale unit is to have pairs of students write stories with the elements of folktales. After the school library media specialist and the classroom teacher model an example together, give each pair of students a sheet with a bare bones outline of the elements:

- Once upon a time . . .
- special people (princess, prince, king, queen)
- three tasks
- evil opponent
- . . . happily ever after

These stories can be illustrated and shared with younger students, or posted on the school or library media center's Web page. The tales may also be written as plays and used for readers' theater or puppet shows. The stories can remain in charted form and made into flannel board stories. This process is started with the library media specialist and continued in the classroom by the teacher. The final products can be performed in the library media center.

Students in grades four, five and six usually prefer to write "fractured" folktales. In the first lesson, read one of the paired books listed below. Chart the plots to show where and when the "fractures" happen. For lesson two, choose a folktale. Chart the events and main characters and, using pair share, have the students write a fractured tale as a whole group. For lesson three, prepare a stack of 10 well-known folktales. Divide the students into groups of four. Each group chooses a story, reads it, charts it, then writes a fractured version of it. If portable keyboards with word processors, such as Dream Writers, are available, have the best typist input the group's ideas. The remainder of the writing should be done in the classroom under the teacher's direction.

> **These stories can be illustrated and shared with younger students or posted on the school or library media center's Web page. The tales may also be written as plays and used for readers' theater or puppet shows.**

▷ TRADITIONAL FOLKTALES AND FRACTURED VERSIONS

- *The Three Bears* by Jan Brett (Dodd, 1987) and *Somebody and the Three Blairs* by Marilyn Tolhurst (Orchard, 1991)
- *Jack and the Beanstalk* by Steven Kellogg (Morrow, 1991) and *Jim and the Beanstalk* by Raymond Briggs (Coward McCann, 1989, 1970)
- *Sleeping Beauty* by Mercer Mayer (Collier, Macmillan, 1984) and *Sleeping Ugly* by Jane Yolen (Coward, McCann, 1981)
- *The Three Pigs* by James Marshall (Dial, 1989) and *The Three Little Wolves and the Big Bad Pig* by Eugene Trivizas (Margaret K. Elderberry, 1993) or *The True Story of the Three Pigs* by Jon Scieszka (Viking Kestrel, 1989)
- *Cinderella* by Paul Galdone (McGraw-Hill, 1978) and *Bubba the Cowboy Prince* by Helen Ketteman (Scholastic, 1997)
- *Twelve Dancing Princesses* by Jane Ray (Dutton, 1996) and *Brothers of the Knight* by Debbie Allen (Dial, 1999)
- *The Little Red Hen* by Paul Galdone (Clarion, 1973) and *Cook-a-doodle-doo* by Janet Stevens (Harcourt Brace, 1999)

The same idea can be applied to the study of genre. Once the criteria for each genre are understood, the library media specialist and the teacher can model how a pair can write the outline for a story of the genre. For example, if science fiction is the chosen genre, the library media specialist and the teacher decide on what scientific principle will be used to create the conflict in the story. They bounce ideas for characters and setting. They chart the story's plot together. The students are then paired, and they follow the model with their own ideas.

◄ CONCLUSION

It is essential that all the writing objectives are modeled several times before students are expected to work independently on the writing activity. Since most of the activities involve pair share, this is an excellent opportunity for the school library media specialist and the teacher to work together as the sample pair. When both people take part in the instruction, the ownership of the activities extends from the library media center to the classroom.

CHAPTER 6

Literary Elements

So many students are able to discuss books using only terms such as "like," "dislike," "exciting," and "funny." When asked to probe further, they are at a loss. The goals of these lessons are deeper reading comprehension, the ability to speak about books in specific terms, and understanding the literary elements in the writing process. The specific objectives are directly related to the NCTE/IRA standards and the SAT 9 test objectives. See Chapter Two for this discussion.

One of the best ways to present literary elements (character, setting, plot, point of view, theme) is by using storytime picture books. They can be read in a short period of time after a concept is introduced. The understanding of the literary elements presented here is partly based on *Aspects of the Novel* by E. M. Forster (Harcourt, 1985, 1927) and *A Critical Handbook of Children's Literature* by Rebecca Lukens (Harper Collins, 1999).

The general lesson design for each of the elements is to teach the basics of the element, then to read picture books that offer clear examples of the element. The library media specialist models the beginning responses. Students, in pairs, are asked to identify the aspects of the element in the picture book. The group comes together to share ideas. Spend at least two lessons on each element for grades one through three. Successive lessons deal with the element being taught and review the elements learned. This provides success and practice in literary analysis. The graphic organizer at the end of the chapter gives students a way to look at books and to write more intelligently about them.

For grades four and above, the second lesson on each element is done with partners. The school library media specialist selects picture books in which the element is easily identifiable. Students read these books in pairs, then complete the recording sheet (recording sheet samples can be found at the end of this chapter). The library media specialist or the teacher can take this information and model how to write an effective paragraph on each element. After this skill is modeled many times, the students can be expected to work in pairs, writing paragraphs about each element. This approach gives students reading and writing practice as well as an opportunity to identify the literary element.

The lessons on each element are alike for a reason. When an effective lesson design remains the same, the students can concentrate on the content.

➤ CHARACTER

Readers know about a character by what he does, says, looks like, and what others and the author say about him. It is helpful to have students describe the library media specialist in this way. Assist the students in making inferences from the specifics. For example, when discussing appearance, if students say the library media specialist wears nice dresses and sneakers, ask what this says about a person. The students will come up with terrific inferences: the library media specialist loves sports, likes to be comfortable, or cannot afford or find nice shoes for her large feet. For traits known by what a character does, students might say the library media specialist smiles and listens to them. Ask what that says about a person. The students will catch on to friendly, kind, and so on, with specifics to back up the generalizations. For traits known by what a character does, students might say "tells stories, helps students find information, and is knowledgeable about good books." This leads to the inferences that the library media specialist is smart, reads a lot, likes kids, and is curious.

> Readers know about a character by what he does, says, looks like, and what others and the author say about him. It is helpful to have students describe the library media specialist in this way.

Read one of the books cited below. Model the analysis the first time by pointing out what the main character was like by what he says, does, looks like, others say about him, and what the author says about the main character.

The next time, review the five ways to know about a character and read another book. Pair the students and ask them to identify character traits. After three or four minutes, pull the group back together and solicit the students' ideas. Charts and graphics can be helpful at this point. A few are included at the end of this chapter.

After a brief introduction to character traits and examples from books previously read, students can delve into more sophisticated ways of discussing character. Characters are "round"—fully fleshed out and capable of surprising the reader—or "flat"—one dimensional. Students learn to identify whether characters in books are round or flat and support their thesis with details from the book. Other aspects of character that can be taught are transformation of a dynamic character (how a character changes in a book) and the interrelation of character and plot (how the character influences the plot and how the plot affects the character). *Pig Pig Grows Up* by David McPhail (Dutton, 1980) is an excellent example of both of these. Another challenging activity is to compare two round characters in a book such as Arnold Lobel's Frog and Toad in *Frog and Toad Are Friends* (HarperCollins, 1971).

LESSON PLANS FOR CHARACTER

Day 1: Introducing character traits

REVIEW: The main character is the one whom the story is about.

OBJECTIVE: The students will demonstrate knowledge of five ways to talk about characters.

DIRECT WHOLE GROUP INSTRUCTION: Tell the students there are at least five ways to understand character. Readers can know about characters by what they look like, what they say, what they do, what others say about them, and what the author says about them. Use recently read books or favorite movies to model inferences about characters.

Ask the students to describe the library media specialist and have them make inferences from the details.

Read *Tacky the Penguin* by Helen Lester.

GUIDED STUDENT PRACTICE: Show the students a few pictures of Tacky. Ask the students to think about what Tacky looked like. After think time, use the pair share strategy from Chapter Four.

Make inferences about Tacky using the details the students have provided about his appearance. Repeat this with what Tacky was like by what he said, did, and others said about him, and rereading sections from the book if students encounter difficulty. Read what the author said about Tacky directly from the book. "Tacky was an odd bird."

CLOSURE: Students chorally respond as the library media specialist pauses as she recites the five ways to talk about a character.

EVALUATION: While the partners share during the student practice, observe whether there are students who do not understand. Circulate and listen to the pairs talking, to evaluate if the students understand the concept of character traits.

Day 2: Reinforcing character traits with grades one, two, and three

REVIEW: There are five ways to talk about character: how a character looks, what he says, what he does, what other characters say about him, and what the author says about the main character.

OBJECTIVE: The students will apply the character traits to a book read aloud.

DIRECT WHOLE GROUP INSTRUCTION: Read *Lilly's Purple Plastic Purse* by Kevin Henkes.

GUIDED STUDENT PRACTICE: Show the students a few pictures of Lilly. Ask the students to think about what Lilly looks like and what that tells the reader about her. After think time, use the pair share strategy.

If students provide details only, question further what those details tell the reader about Lilly. Repeat this with what Lilly was like by what she said, did, and others said about her, rereading sections from the book if students encounter difficulty. Read what the author said about Lilly directly from the book.

CLOSURE: Students offer inferences about Lilly.

EVALUATION: While the partners share during the student practice, observe whether there are students who do not understand. Circulate and listen to the pairs talking, to evaluate if the students understand the concept of character traits.

Day 2: Reinforcing character traits with grades four, five, and six

REVIEW: There are five ways to talk about character: how a character looks, what he says, what he does, what other characters say about him, and what the author says about the main character.

OBJECTIVE: The students will apply the character traits to a book they read aloud to a partner.

DIRECT WHOLE GROUP INSTRUCTION: Using an overhead projector, white board, or smart board, model how to fill out the recording sheet that the students will use. Use the previous day's story as the example.

GUIDED STUDENT PRACTICE: Students are paired and given a picture book that clearly shows character traits. They read the book together, then record what the main character was like by what the character looked like, said, did, what others said about the character and what the author said. Circulate among the students. If a pair provides details only, question further what those details tell the reader about the main character.

CLOSURE: The pairs share their inferences about the characters in the books.

EVALUATION: Use the recording sheet and oral responses for summative evaluation. The day 2 lesson on each literary element for grades four, five, and six follows the same model. Examples of recording sheets are included at the end of the chapter.

Day 3: Writing lesson for grades four, five, and six

REVIEW: There are five ways to talk about character: how a character looks, what he says, what he does, what other characters say about him, and what the author says about the main character.

OBJECTIVE: The students will use the recording sheets from day 2 to write a paragraph about the main character in the book they read the preceding day.

DIRECT WHOLE GROUP INSTRUCTION: Using an overhead projector, white board, or smart board, model how to use the information on the recording sheet to write a cogent paragraph. Use the previous day's recording sheet as the example. Make sure that the topic sentence reflects an inference about the character. The inference should be supported by the details of what the character looked like, did, and said; and what others and the author said about him or her.

For instance, if *Julius, the Baby of the World*, by Kevin Henkes (Greenwillow, 1990) is used, the topic sentence might be "Lilly was jealous of her new brother Julius, and didn't like him." The sentences with supporting details might be "She left the baby out of the family portrait. She tried to make him disappear. She said she hated Julius. She was supposed to teach him the alphabet, but she said the letters in the wrong order; Her parents put her in the uncooperative chair when she told the story of Julius, the germ of the world. The author wants the reader to know that Lilly was the best sister in the world before Julius was born when he writes that she told him secrets and sang lullabies to him every night." The practice can be further modeled by creating a second paragraph about how Lilly changed after her cousin made fun of the baby.

GUIDED STUDENT PRACTICE: Students reread their comments from the day before and write a paragraph together, based on the information. The book read should be available for consultation during this process.

CLOSURE: Select several of the pairs to read their paragraphs, pointing out the topic sentence and supporting details.

EVALUATION: Formative evaluation is based on the observation of the pairs, as the process is ongoing. Summative evaluation is based on the paragraphs, and whether they meet the criteria of a topic sentence and supporting sentences with details that have inferences about the character.

Day 3: (Alternative) Writing products based on literary elements for grades four, five, and six

REVIEW: There are five ways to talk about character: how a character looks, what he says, what he does, what other characters say about him, and what the author says about the main character.

OBJECTIVE: The students will apply the character traits to create a character sketch with a partner.

DIRECT WHOLE GROUP INSTRUCTION: Using an overhead projector, white board, or smart board, model how to create a "round," fully realized, character. Describe a situation, such as a classroom, where the teacher is absent and there is a substitute. The assignment is to make up a character and tell what he or she would do in the situation. Give the character a "personality" by describing the physical attributes, how he or she treats the substitute and other students in words and actions, and what the other students and the substitute say about the character. Model the assignment by making up a student and naming him or her. Describe what he or she looks like. Create his or her reaction to the substitute (helpful, disruptive, scared, and so on) and spoken reactions of other students and the substitute.

GUIDED STUDENT PRACTICE: In pairs, students brainstorm the same assignment. After they discuss it, one in each pair records the character sketch.

CLOSURE: Students share their character sketches, pointing out the way the character is revealed by appearance, actions, words, and what others say about the character.

The students should have time in the classroom to polish the character sketches if a finished product is desired. Make sure the students know that the library media specialist will read the finished products. The library media specialist may want to assist the teacher in the evaluation of the paragraphs.

Titles that emphasize character

Allard, Harry, *Miss Nelson is Missing.* Houghton Mifflin, 1977.

DeGroat, Diane, *Roses are Pink, Your Feet Really Stink.* Mulberry, 1977.

De Paola, Tomie, *Strega Nona.* Prentice Hall, 1975.

Gantos, Jack, *Rotten Ralph's Rotten Romance.* Houghton Mifflin, 1997.

Goble, Paul, *The Girl Who Loved Wild Horses.* Aladdin, 1976.

Graves, Keith, *Frank Was a Monster Who Wanted to Dance.* Chronicle, 1999.

Greenfield, Louise, *She Come Bringing Me That Little Baby.* HarperCollins, 1993.

Henkes, Kevin, *Chrysanthemum.* Greenwillow, 1991.

Henkes, Kevin, *Julius, the Baby of the World.* Greenwillow, 1990.

Henkes, Kevin, *Lilly's Purple Plastic Purse.* Greenwillow, 1996.

Hoban, Lillian, *Arthur's Great Big Valentine.* HarperCollins, 1989.

Hoban, Russell, *Bread and Jam for Frances.* HarperCollins, 1964.

Hoffman, Mary, *Amazing Grace.* Dial, 1991.

Kraus, Robert, *Leo the Late Bloomer.* Simon & Schuster, 1971.

Lester, Helen, *Tacky the Penguin.* Houghton Mifflin, 1988.

Lionni, Leo, *Frederick.* Knopf, 1987,1967.

Lobel, Arnold, *Frog and Toad Together.* HarperCollins, 1971.

London, Jonathan, *Froggy Plays Soccer.* Viking, 1999

Loredo, Elizabeth, *Boogie Bones.* Putnam's, 1997.

Low, Joseph, *Mice Twice.* Atheneum, 1980.

Marshall, James, *George and Martha.* Houghton Mifflin, 1972.

Marshall, James, *The Cut-Ups.* Puffin, 1986.

McKee, David, *Elmer.* Lothrop, 1989.

McKissick, Pat, *Flossie and the Fox.* Dial, 1986.

McPhail, David, *Pig Pig Grows Up.* Dutton, 1980.

Mora, Pat, *Tomas and the Library Lady.* Knopf, 1997.

Potter, Beatrix, *Peter Rabbit.* Little Simon, 1986.

Prigger, Mary Skillings, *Aunt Minnie McGranahan.* Clarion, 1999.

Rahaman, Vashanti, *Read for Me, Mama.* Boyds Mills, 1997.

Rey, H.A., *Curious George.* Houghton Mifflin, 1973, 1941.

San Souci, *A Weave of Words.* Orchard, 1998.

Sendak, Maurice, *Pierre.* HarperCollins, 1990, 1962.

Shannon, George, *Lizard's Song.* Mulberry, 1992, 1981.

Soto, Gary, *Chato's Kitchen.* Putnam, 1997.

Steig, William, *Dr. DeSoto.* Scholastic, 1982.

Steptoe, John, *Stevie.* Harper & Row, 1969.

Williams, Suzanne, *Library Lil.* Dial, 1997.

▷ SETTING

Setting is the time and place of a book. For young children, this can be labeled the "when" and "where." Holiday stories are usually good examples of specific times and places. For older readers, the element of setting can be more complex. Setting can be "backdrop" where it doesn't much matter what the setting is, or "integral" where the setting is fully entwined with the other elements. It can show the reader something important about the character, as it does for Mr. Moose in Eve Bunting's *A Turkey for Thanksgiving* (Clarion, 1991). The setting can be the antagonist. Nazi Germany is the hostile setting for a Jewish child in J. Hoestalandt's *Star of Fear, Star of Hope* (Walker, 1995). The setting of Valentine's Day in *Roses Are Pink, Your Feet Really Stink* by Diane DeGroat (Morrow, 1996) points out the conflicts among students. The Sheriff's character becomes clearer as he ventures into the desert to search for an orphan in Diane Stanley's *Saving Sweetness* (Putnam, 1996).

LESSON PLANS FOR SETTING

Day 1: Introducing setting

REVIEW: There are five ways to talk about characters.

OBJECTIVE: The students will verbally demonstrate knowledge that the setting is the time and place of a story.

DIRECT WHOLE GROUP INSTRUCTION: Tell the students that the setting is the time and place of a story. Ask the students to describe their present setting (the library media center, in a school, contemporary). Model applying the concept of setting by relating it to the book read aloud the day before. Read *Lost,* by Paul Brett Johnson (Orchard, 1996), or another book that emphasizes setting.

GUIDED STUDENT PRACTICE: Show the students a few of the book's pictures. Review that setting is the time and place of a story. Ask the students to think about the setting of the book read. After think time, use pair share. Extend the lesson by modeling responses about the function of the setting as the antagonist. The desert was the enemy of the dog because he did not know how to get food, water, or shelter.

CLOSURE: Ask the students to chorally respond to the questions, "What was the setting for the dog? What was the setting for the family?"

Day 2: Reinforcing setting with grades one, two, and three

REVIEW: The setting is the time and place of the book.

OBJECTIVE: The students will apply the concept of setting to a book read aloud.

DIRECT WHOLE GROUP INSTRUCTION: Read *The Biggest Bear* by Lynd Ward and *The Gardener* by Sarah Stewart, both cited in the bibliography.

GUIDED STUDENT PRACTICE: Ask the students to identify the setting of each story. After think time, use the pair share strategy from Chapter Four.

After students have identified the settings, introduce the function of setting. Not all students will grasp the concept, but some will. Model the response on how the setting in *The Biggest Bear* spells out the conflict—that a wild animal cannot be expected to live with people. Model the response on how the setting in *The Gardener* points out the girl's character in that she wanted to please her uncle and use her gardening skills to make the city beautiful and more like home.

CLOSURE: Students chorally respond to the question, "What is a setting in a story?"

Day 2 for grades four, five, and six is the same format as the one on character. The recording sheet is included at the end of this chapter.

Day 3: Writing lesson for grades four, five, and six

REVIEW: The setting is the time and place of a story.

OBJECTIVE: The students will use the recording sheets from day 2 to write a paragraph about the setting in the book they read the preceding day.

DIRECT WHOLE GROUP INSTRUCTION: Using an overhead projector, white board, or smart board, model how to use the information on the recording sheet to write a cogent paragraph.

Use the previous day's recording sheet as the example. Make sure that the topic sentence is a general statement of the time or place of the book. The supporting sentences should include further details of the setting. For example, if *A Woggle of Witches* by Adrienne Adams (Scribners, 1971) is used, the topic sentence might be *"A Woggle of Witches* takes place in the forest, in the sky, and in a cornfield on Halloween night." The sentences with supporting details might be "The witches live a forest that has many tall trees. They fly on their broomsticks up to the moon. They land in a cornfield. The reader knows it is Halloween because the witches are frightened by children who are dressed up for trick or treating."

GUIDED STUDENT PRACTICE: Students reread their comments on their recording sheet from the day before and write a paragraph together, based on the information. The book read should be available for consultation during this process.

CLOSURE: Select several of the pairs to read their paragraphs, pointing out the topic sentence and supporting details.

EVALUATION: Formative evaluation is based on the observation of the pairs, as the process is ongoing. Summative evaluation is based on the paragraphs and whether they meet the criteria.

Day 3: (Alternative) Writing products based on literary elements for grades four, five, and six

REVIEW: The setting is the time and place of a story.

OBJECTIVE: The students will write a 20-second "commercial" describing a setting they've made up.

DIRECT WHOLE GROUP INSTRUCTION: Using an overhead projector, white board, or smart board, model how to create setting. The assignment is to describe a specific type of place, such as a scary one, another planet, or one based on a social studies unit the class is studying, and so on. Describe what it looks like and the time (current, a specific time in the past, a specific time of year, etc.). For instance, if the class is studying Ancient Egypt, write a description of work on the pyramids. If the assignment is to be an imaginary place, brainstorm ideas, then write a paragraph describing the place.

GUIDED STUDENT PRACTICE: In pairs, students brainstorm the same assignment. After they discuss it, one in each pair records the "commercial" of the setting.

EVALUATION: Students share their commercials, pointing out the details of the time and place.

Titles that emphasize setting

Adams, Adrienne, *A Woggle of Witches.* Scribners, 1971.
Bunting, Eve, *Train to Somewhere.* Clarion, 1996.
Bunting, Eve, *A Turkey for Thanksgiving.* Clarion, 1991.
Cannon, Janell, *Stellaluna.* Harcourt, 1993.
DeGroat, Diane, *Roses are Pink, Your Feet Really Stink.* Morrow, 1996.
Galdone, Paul, *The Three Bears.* Clarion, 1972.
Hoban, Lillian, *Arthur's Big Valentine.* Harper Trophy, 1991.
Hoestalandt, J., *Star of Fear, Star of Hope.* Walker, 1995.
Johnson, Paul Brett, *Lost.* Orchard, 1996.
Kimmel, Eric, *Herschel and the Hanukkah Goblins.* Holiday House, 1989.
Lester, Julius, *Black Cowboy, Wild Horses.* Dial, 1988.

Lewin, Betsy, *What's the Matter, Habibi?* Clarion, 1997.

Lewin, Hugh, *Jafta and the Wedding.* Carolrhoda, 1983, 1981.

Lewin, Ted, *The Storytellers.* Lothrop, 1998.

London, Jonathan, *Froggy Gets Dressed.* Viking, 1992.

McCloskey, Robert, *Make Way for Ducklings.* Viking, 1969.

McLerran, Alice, *Roxaboxen.* Lothrop, 1990.

McLerran, Alice, *The Year of the Ranch.* Viking, 1996.

McPhail, David, *Farm Morning.* Harcourt, 1985.

Martin, Jacqueline Briggs, *Snowflake Bentley.* Houghton Mifflin, 1998.

Mayer, Mercer, *Liza Lou and the Yeller Belly Swamp.* Four Winds, 1980, 1976.

Moss, Marissa, *True Heart.* Silverwhistle, San Diego, 1999.

Nerlove, Miriam, *Flowers on the Wall.* Margaret K. Elderberry, 1996.

Noble, Trinka Hakes, *The Day Jimmy's Boa Ate the Wash.* Dial, 1980.

Raczek, Linda Theresa, *The Night the Grandfathers Danced.* Northland, 1995.

Seuling, Barbara, *Winter Lullaby.* Harcourt, 1998.

Sharmat, Marjorie Wienman, *Gila Monsters Meet You at the Airport.* Puffin, 1983.

Soto, Gary, *Too Many Tamales.* Putnam, 1996.

Stanley, Diane, *Saving Sweetness.* Putnam, 1996.

Stewart, Sarah, *The Gardener.* Farrar, 1997.

Tamar, Erika, *The Garden of Happiness.* Harcourt, 1996.

Ward, Lynd, *The Biggest Bear.* Houghton, 1988, 1952.

Wellington, Monica, *Night City.* Dutton, 1998.

Wiesner, David, *Tuesday.* Clarion, 1991.

Winch, John, *The Old Woman Who Loved to Read.* Holiday, 1997.

▶ PLOT

Plot is the sequence of events that shows the character in action. Most books have a conflict, a problem that needs to be resolved. The best introduction is to use a book that has an obvious sequence of events and obvious problems. These should be tackled in different lessons for primary students.

Take the study of plot one step further for older students. Discuss the four types of conflicts: person against himself, person against person, person against society, and person against nature. For example, in *Mean Soup* by Betsy Everitt (Voyager/Harcourt, 1992), the conflict is person against himself. The boy is angry and upset. His mother helps him to restore his inner peace. Person against person involves the main character in a struggle with an antagonist. In *Borreguita and the Coyote* by Verna Aardema (Knopf, 1991), the coyote is the antagonist against the little sheep, the main character. The person against society conflict can be seen in *The Sneetches* by Dr. Seuss (Random, 1989, 1961), where one group makes rules that are detrimental to other groups. One of the conflicts in *Swimmy* by Leo Lionni (Pantheon, 1963) is "person" against nature. It is a law of nature that small fish like Swimmy aand his siblings are eaten by larger fish.

Sometimes the conflict may fit into several categories. This makes for lively and interesting discussions, forcing the students to back up their answers with specifics from the story.

LESSON PLANS FOR PLOT

Day 1: Introducing plot as the sequence of events

REVIEW: There are five ways to talk about characters, and the setting is the time and place of a story.

OBJECTIVE: The students will demonstrate knowledge of plot as the sequence of events in a story and will be able to put the main events of a story in correct sequence.

DIRECT WHOLE GROUP INSTRUCTION: Tell the students that the plot is the sequence of events of a story, the order in which things happen. Explain the concept by using examples of a morning routine: "I wake up. I take a shower. I go to school." Change the order of these, and the students will recognize what a rational sequence is. Model how to apply this concept by going over the sequence of events in one of the stories read the day before. Read *Where the Wild Things Are* by Maurice Sendak (or another book that accentuates sequence of events).

GUIDED STUDENT PRACTICE: Show the students a few of the book's pictures. Review that plot is the sequence of events in a story. Ask the students to think about the plot of the book read and to put four main events in order. Provide pictures, sentence cards, or a chart with the four events. If the chart is used, have the students mentally put the event in order. Have them show, by using the fingers of their raised hands, which event came first.

CLOSURE: Ask the students to chorally respond to the questions "Which came first in the story? Next? Next? And which came last?"

EVALUATION: If the students have sentence cards or pictures, observe as they put them in order. Circulate and listen to the pairs talking, to evaluate if the students understand the concept of sequencing events.

Day 2: Plot as problem and solution for grades one, two, and three

REVIEW: The plot is the sequence of events. Model the application of the concepts of the setting and characters in the books read the day before.

OBJECTIVE: The students will apply the concept of problem and solution to a book read aloud.

DIRECT WHOLE GROUP INSTRUCTION: Relate problem and solution to an incident on the playground or in the library. Read *Swimmy* by Leo Lionni and *Goggles* by Ezra Jack Keats.

GUIDED STUDENT PRACTICE: After each book is read, ask the students to identify the problem and solution in each story. After think time, use the pair share to elicit responses.

After students have identified the problems and solutions, introduce (for grades two and three) the concept of the types of conflicts. Not all students will grasp the concept, but some will. Model responses on conflict using *Swimmy* (person against nature, that it is a law of nature that big fish eat little fish) and *Goggles* (person against person, Peter against the boys who want his goggles). Use examples from books recently read to model the conflicts of person against himself and person against society. *David Goes to School* by David Small (Scholastic, 1999) is an excellent example of the latter.

CLOSURE: Students offer their ideas about problems and solutions in another book recently read aloud.

Day 2 for grades four, five, and six is the same format as the one on character. A recording sheet example is included at the end of this chapter.

Day 3: Writing lesson for grades four, five, and six

REVIEW: There are four types of conflicts: person against person, person against himself or herself, person against society, and person against nature.

OBJECTIVE: The students will use the recording sheets from day 2 to write a paragraph about the conflict in the book they read the preceding day.

DIRECT WHOLE GROUP INSTRUCTION: Using an overhead projector, white board, or smart board, model how to use the information on the recording sheet to write a cogent paragraph. Use the previous day's recording sheet as the example. Make sure that the topic sentence is a general statement of the type of conflict in the book. The supporting sentences should include who is in conflict and why. For example, if *Click, Clack, Moo: Cows That Type* by Doreen Cronin (Simon & Schuster, 2000) is used, the topic sentence might be "The conflict in *Click, Clack, Moo: Cows That Type* is person against person." The sentences with supporting details might be "The cows find an old typewriter and use it to issue demands to Farmer Brown. He wants them to produce milk. They want electric blankets. The conflict is solved when Farmer Brown gives the cows electric blankets, and the cows give him milk and the typewriter back."

GUIDED STUDENT PRACTICE: Students reread their comments on their recording sheet from the day before and write a paragraph together, based on the information. The book read should be available for consultation during this process.

CLOSURE: Select several pairs to read their paragraphs, pointing out the type of conflict, who the conflict involved, and how it was resolved.

Day 3: (Alternative) Writing products based on literary elements for grades four, five, and six

REVIEW: There are four types of conflicts: person against person, person against himself or herself, person against society, and person against nature.

OBJECTIVE: The students will write a paragraph describing a conflict.

DIRECT WHOLE GROUP INSTRUCTION: Using an overhead projector, white board, or smart board, model how to create a conflict in a story. The assignment is to describe a type of conflict. Try to relate the assignment to a content area the students are studying. Identify the type of conflict, who is involved, and a resolution. For example, if the class is studying weather, model a conflict of person against nature. For example, two children are home alone when a thunderstorm strikes. If the class is studying a specific period of history, model a paragraph of the conflict from the issues of that time, such as a Native American and a prospector in the Southwest.

GUIDED STUDENT PRACTICE: In pairs, students brainstorm the same assignment. After they discuss it, one in each pair records the conflict.

CLOSURE: Students share their paragraphs on a conflict, pointing out the type, the participants, and the resolution.

Titles that emphasize plot and conflict

Aardema, Verna, *Borreguita and the Coyote.* Knopf, 1991.

Browne, Anthony, *The Piggybook.* Knopf, 1986.

Cole, Joanna, *Bony-Legs.* Scholastic, 1983.

Cronin, Doreen, *Click, Clack, Moo: Cows That Type.* Simon & Schuster, 2000.

Diakite, Baba Wague, *The Hatseller and the Monkeys.* Scholastic, 1999.

Everitt, Betsy, *Mean Soup.* Voyager/Harcourt, 1992.

Hazen, Barbara, *Tight Times.* Puffin, 1983.

Henkes, Kevin, *Owen.* Greenwillow, 1993.

Hest, Amy, *When Jessie Came Across the Sea.* Candlewick, 1997.

Johnston, Tony, *Alice Nizzy Nazzy, the Witch of Sante Fe.* Putnam, 1998.

Kasza, Keiko, *Wolf's Chicken Soup.* Putnam, 1996.

Keats, Ezra Jack, *Goggles.* Viking, 1998.

Kvasnosky, Laura McGee, *Zelda and Ivy.* Candlewick, 1998.

Lionni, Leo, *Swimmy.* Pantheon, 1963.

McKissack, Pat. *Flossie and the Fox.* Dial, 1986.

Mayer, Mercer, *Liza Lou and the Yeller Belly Swamp.* Four Winds, 1976.

Meddaugh, Susan, *Hog-Eye.* Houghton Mifflin, 1995.

Ness, Evaline, *Sam, Bangs and Moonshine.* Holt, 1966.

San Souci, Robert, *The Faithful Friend.* Simon & Schuster, 1995.

Seeger, Pete, *Abiyoyo.* Simon & Schuster, 1986.

Sendak, Maurice, *Where the Wild Things Are.* HarperCollins, 1984, 1963.

Seuss, Dr., *How the Grinch Stole Christmas.* Random, 1957.

Seuss, Dr., *The Grinch Who Stole Christmas.* Random, 1957.

Seuss, Dr., *The Sneetches and Other Stories.* Random, 1989, 1961.

Shannon, George, *Dance Away.* Greenwillow, 1982.

Small, David, *David Goes to School.* Blue Sky Press, 1999.

Small, David, *No, David !* Blue Sky Press, 1998.

Soto, Gary, *Too Many Tamales.* Putnam, 1996.

Trivizas, Eugene, *Three Little Wolves and the Big Bad Pig.* Aladdin Paperbacks, 1993.

Turkle, Brinton, *Do not Open.* Dutton, 1985.

Wells, Rosemary, *Bunny Cakes.* Dial, 1997.

Wilhelm, Hans, *Tyrone the Horrible.* Scholastic, 1988.

Williams, Vera B., *A Chair for My Mother.* Mulberry, 1988, 1982.

Woodruff, Elvira, *The Memory Coat.* Scholastic 1999.

⊳ THEME

Theme is the underlying idea of a book. It is what the author wants the reader to think about afterwards. It is the meaning of the book. Usually it is a comment on the human condition. Themes can be explicit, meaning they are stated right in the text. Themes can also be implicit, implied by the words, action, and subtext. There is always a primary or main theme. Stick with these for the younger students. Remember that readers bring their own personal experiences to books, so they may interpret themes differently. There are many "right" answers when dealing with them, but there are also wrong answers because they cannot be supported by the story.

Students often confuse theme with main idea. It is useful to teach both at the same time so the difference is obvious. The main idea is what the book is about rather than the meaning of the story.

LESSON PLAN

⭐ LESSON PLANS FOR THEME

Day 1: Introducing theme and main idea

REVIEW: Reiterate the ways to talk about characters, setting, and plot

OBJECTIVE: The students will identify the theme and the main idea of a story.

DIRECT WHOLE GROUP INSTRUCTION: Tell the students that the main idea is what the story is about. The theme is the idea behind the story. Model applying the concepts of main idea and theme by relating them to the book read aloud the day before. Read *The Runaway Bunny* by Margaret Wise Brown (Harper, 1972, 1942) or another book that accentuates the difference between theme and main idea.

GUIDED STUDENT PRACTICE: Use pair share to elicit the main idea (a young bunny thinks of ways to escape his mother). Model the application of theme (the mother will always be connected and love her child), then ask if anyone picked up a different theme. Read *Claude the Dog* by Dick Gackenback (Seabury, 1974). Use pair share to elicit the main idea and the theme.

CLOSURE: Identify the main ideas and themes of the two books read.

Day 2 for grades one, two, and three is a repeat of the first lesson with different stories read aloud.

Day 2 for grades four, five, and six is the same format as the one on character. The recording sheet is included at the end of this chapter.

Day 3: Writing lesson for grades four, five, and six

REVIEW: The main idea is what the story is about. The theme is the idea that the author wants the reader to consider after reading the story.

OBJECTIVE: The students will use the recording sheets from day 2 to write a paragraph about the theme and the main idea in the book they read the preceding day.

DIRECT WHOLE GROUP INSTRUCTION: Using an overhead projector, white board, or smart board, model how to use the information on the recording sheet to write a cogent paragraph. Use the previous day's recording sheet as the example. Make sure that the topic sentence is a statement about the main idea of the book. The next sentence should state the theme. The supporting sentences should explain the theme. For example, if *Officer Buckle and Gloria* by Peggy Rathman (Putnam, 1995) is used, the first sentence might be "*Officer Buckle and Gloria* is about a police officer who gives boring and ineffective safety speeches until he teams up with a police dog, Gloria." The sentence with the rest of the main idea could be "Officer Buckle gets jealous when he realizes that the audiences are responding to the dog, not him. He finally decides to work with Gloria because the message gets across to the students." There are many possible theme sentences. One could be "The theme of the book is that each person has a talent that can be used for good, and that together people can do even better things." The supporting sentences might be "Officer Buckle knew all the safety tips, but Gloria knew how to make students listen and understand them. Each by themselves couldn't do the job. They needed to cooperate."

GUIDED STUDENT PRACTICE: Students should reread their comments on their recording sheet from the day before and write a paragraph together, based on the information. The book read should be available for consultation during this process.

CLOSURE: Select several of the pairs to read their paragraphs, pointing out the main idea and the theme.

Titles that emphasize theme

Altman, Linda Jacobs, *The Legend of Freedom Hill*. Lee & Low, 2000.
Brown, Margaret Wise, *The Runaway Bunny*. Harper, 1972, 1942.
Casler, Leigh, *The Boy Who Dreamed of an Acorn*. Philomel, 1994.
Clifton, Lucille, *Everett Anderson's Friend*. Holt, 1992.
Coursen, Valerie, *Mordant's Wish*. Holt, 1997.
Demi, *The Empty Pot*. Holt, 1990.
Eduar, Gilles, *Jooka Saves the Day*. Orchard, 1997.
Egan, Tim, *Metropolitan Cow*. Houghton, 1996.
Ernst, Lisa Campbell, *Zinnia and Dot*. Viking, 1992.
Everitt, Betsy, *Mean Soup*. Harcourt, 1992.
Fine, Edith Hope, *Under the Lemon Tree*. Lee & Lothrop, 1999.
Gackenback, Dick, *Claude the Dog*. Seabury, 1974.
Haas, Jesse, *Busybody Brandy*. Greenwillow, 1990.
Henkes, Kevin, *Julius, the Baby of the World*. Greenwillow, 1990.
Isadora, Rachel, *Max*. Collier, 1984, 1976.
Jackson, Isaac, *Somebody's New Pajamas*. Dial, 1996.
Johnston, Tony, *Sparky and Eddie: Wild, Wild Rodeo*. Scholastic, 1998.
Joose, Barbara, *Mama, Do You Love Me?* Chronicle, 1991.
Lewin, Hugh, *Jafta's Father*. Carolrhoda, 1983, 1981.
Lionni, Leo, *Frederick*. Pantheon, 1967.
McCourt, Lisa, *I Miss you, Stinky Face*. Troll, 1999.
Mitchell, Lori, *Different Just Like Me*. Charlesbridge, 1999.
Rathman, Peggy, *Officer Buckle and Gloria*. Putnam, 1995.
Scheffler, Ursel, *Who Has Time for Little Bear?* Doubleday, 1998.
Williams, Vera B., *A Chair for My Mother*. Greenwillow, 1982.
Yorinks, Arthur, *Hey, Al*. Farrar, 1986.
Young, Ed, *Seven Blind Mice*. Philomel, 1992.

▶ POINT OF VIEW

The point of view is through whose eyes and mind the reader sees the action in a book. The first person point of view is when "I" is telling the story. There are very few books written in the second person, "you." The third person is when "he," "she," or "they" are telling the story.

In the third person point of view, there are interesting differences. The "omniscient" point of view is when the reader is inside each of the character's thoughts. Students as young as second grade love to be able to use the word "omniscient" appropriately.

The "limited omniscient" point of view is when the story is told in the third person but through the eyes and mind of one or two characters. How the action is seen is colored by the character traits of the narrator. Students enjoy the twists in an unreliable narrator, like the Sheriff in *Saving Sweetness* by Diane Stanley (Putnam, 1996). Certainly, A. Wolf's version of *The True Story of the Three Little Pigs* by Jon Sceiszka (Viking, 1989) differs dramatically from the folktale version.

LESSON PLAN

LESSON PLANS FOR POINT OF VIEW

Day 1: Introducing point of view

REVIEW: Reiterate the ways to talk about characters, setting, plot, main idea, and theme.

OBJECTIVE: The students will identify the point of view of a book read aloud.

RATIONALE: It makes a big difference in reading fiction or nonfiction as to who is writing or telling the story.

DIRECT WHOLE GROUP INSTRUCTION: Explain the differences between first, second, and third person. Model applying the concept of point of view by relating it to the book read aloud the day before. Read short books with the first and third person point of view. Extend the learning by addressing the concepts of omniscient and limited omniscient.

GUIDED STUDENT PRACTICE: Review first and third person. Ask the students to think about the book read and who was telling the story. After think time, use pair share.

CLOSURE: Ask the students to chorally respond to the questions, "In which story was 'I' telling the story?" "That is a first person story." "In which story was 'he' telling the story?" "That is a third person story."

Day 2 for grades one, two, and three is a repeat of the first lesson with different stories read aloud.

Day 2 for grades four, five, and six is the same format as the one on character. The recording sheet is included at the end of this chapter.

Day 3: Writing lessons on point of view for grades, three, four, five, and six

REVIEW: Reiterate the meaning of first and third person point of view, both limited omniscient and omniscient.

OBJECTIVE: Students will change a well-known story by making the narrator the antagonist of the story.

DIRECT WHOLE GROUP INSTRUCTION: Read or tell a short traditional tale: *The Three Bears, The Gingerbread Boy, Red Riding Hood, The Three Wishes,* or *The Musicians of Brementown*, all cited on page 42. Model how the story would be different if narrated in the first person by the antagonist. For example, if *The Gingerbread Boy* is chosen, change the story by telling it from the old woman's point of view: "My husband and I don't have any children. One day, while I was baking gingerbread cookies, I sculpted a boy. I put two fine fat currants for the eyes, a chocolate chip for the nose, a red hot candy for the mouth, and icing for a jacket. I put him in the oven to bake. When it was time for him to be done, I opened the oven door. Out jumped my gingerbread boy! Gave me the scare of my life! My husband and I chased him across the room but he ran out the door. How I wanted that little gingerbread boy! He taunted and teased me by saying, 'Run, run, as fast as you can, you can't catch me, I'm the gingerbread man.'"

GUIDED STUDENT PRACTICE: Have the students offer suggestions for the new version.

CLOSURE: Read a paragraph from the original story and tell the same incident from the other narrator's point of view.

Day 4: Writing Lesson on Point of View and Folktales

REVIEW: The traditional folktales would be different if written from another characater's viewpoint.

OBJECTIVE: Students will change a well-known story by making the narrator the antagonist of the story.

DIRECT WHOLE GROUP INSTRUCTION: Read or tell a short traditional tale: *The Three Bears, The Gingerbread Boy, Red Riding Hood, The Three Wishes, The Musicians of Brementown,* or *The Magic Porridge Pot,* all cited in the bibliography.

GUIDED STUDENT PRACTICE: Divide the students into groups by the main characters in the conflict. For example, if *The Three Bears* is used, assign half of the groups to write as Goldilocks and half of the groups to write as the baby bear. Have each group discuss what the story would be like from that character's point of view. Have each group compose the bare bones of the story. Have one person be the recorder.

CLOSURE: Have the recorders tell the new stories.

Titles that emphasize point of view

Buchanan, Ken, *This House Is Made of Mud.* Northland,1991.

Cohen, Miriam, *Will I Have a Friend?* Simon & Schuster, 1967.

Domanska, Janina, *Marilka.* Macmillan, 1970.

Galdone, Paul, *Little Red Hen.* Clarion, 1973.

Galdone, Paul, *The Magic Porridge Pot.* Houghton Miffin, 1976.

Gelman, Rita Golden, *I Went to the Zoo.* Scholastic, 1993.

Graham, Bob, *Crusher Is Coming.* Viking, 1988.

Greenfield, Eloise, *Me and Neesie.* Crowell, 1975.

Havill, Jaunita, *Jamaica Tag-Along.* Houghton Mifflin, 1989.

Hayes, Joe, *The Soft Child.* Roberts Rhinehart, 1993.

Hort, Lenny, *How Many Stars in the Sky?* Mulberry, 1997.

Keats, Ezra Jack, *Whistle for Willie.* Viking, 1964.

Krensky, Stephen, *My Teacher's Secret Life.* Simon & Schuster, 1996.

Kroll, Virginia, *Faraway Drums.* Little, Brown, 1998.

Lobel, Arnold, *On Market Street.* Greenwillow, 1981.

Lewin, Hugh, *Jafta's Mother.* Carolrhoda, 1983, 1981.

Marshall, James, *Yummers!* Houghton Mifflin, 1972.

McAllister, Angela, *The Snow Angel.* Lothrop, 1993.

Pinkwater, Daniel M., *I Was a Second Grade Werewolf.* Dutton, 1983.

Rylant, Cynthia, *When I Was Young in the Mountains.* Dutton, 1982.

Sceiszka, Jon, *The True Story of the Three Little Pigs.* Viking, 1989.

Trivizas, Eugenios, *The Three Little Wolves and the Big Bad Pig.* Margaret K. Elderberry, 1993.

Wood, Audrey. *King Bidgood's in the Bathtub.* Harcourt, 1985.

Yolen, Jane, *The Musicians of Bremen.* Simon & Schuster, 1996.

CULMINATING LESSON FOR GRADES FOUR, FIVE, AND SIX
STORY QUILTS: INTEGRATING ALL THE LITERARY ELEMENTS

REVIEW: Reiterate the meanings of the literary elements of character, setting, plot, theme, and point of view.

OBJECTIVE: Students will identify these elements and make a story quilt about a story read aloud.

DIRECT WHOLE GROUP INSTRUCTION: Read one of the titles from the bibliographies in the other literary element lessons.

GUIDED PRACTICE: Divide the students into groups of five. Give specific instructions on how to do the story quilt. The story quilt idea is part of a teacher workshop in Lesley S. J. Farmer's *Workshops for Teachers: Becoming Partners for Information Literacy* (Linworth, 1995). Each group gets eleven squares, each of which is labeled setting, character, beginning sequence of events, middle sequence of events, ending sequence of events, conflict, point of view, theme, main idea, title and author. The students write the information on these squares, then illustrate them. The squares are glued on pre-cut butcher paper and displayed in the classroom, library, office, cafeteria, or hallway.

CLOSURE: Have students show and explain their quilts to each other.

Note: This lesson may take more than one class period.

Worksheets and Graphic Organizers

STUDENTS' NAMES _____

BOOK TITLE _____

Who is the main character?

Describe the main character by what he or she looks like.

What is the main character like by what he or she says?

What is the main character like by what he or she does?

What is the main character like by what others say about him or her?

What is the main character like by what the author says about him or her?

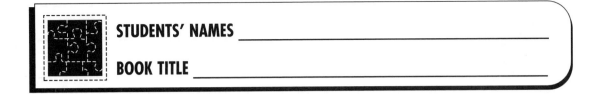

STUDENTS' NAMES _____

BOOK TITLE _____

Describe the time of the setting:

Describe the place of the setting:

Why is the setting important?

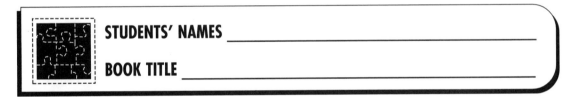

STUDENTS' NAMES _____

BOOK TITLE _____

Describe the point of view (through whose eyes do you see the story?)

Who is it?

first person?   third person?   omniscient?

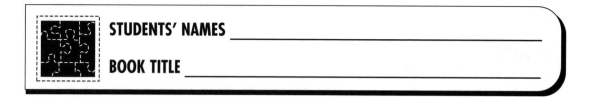

STUDENTS' NAMES _____

BOOK TITLE _____

Describe the problem (conflict):

Is it person against person, person against himself/herself, person against nature or person against society?

Who is against what or whom?

Why?

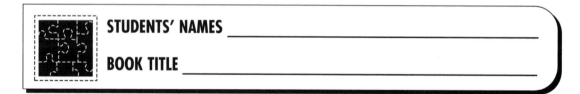

STUDENTS' NAMES _____

BOOK TITLE _____

What is the main idea? (what is the book about?)

What is the theme? (what does the author want you think about after you finish the story?

TITLE _____

MAIN CHARACTER _____

     by appearance _____

     words _____

     deeds _____

     what others think _____

     what the author thinks _____

SETTING _____

     time _____ place _____

CONFLICT _____

     type _____

     who _____

MAIN IDEA _____

_____

THEME _____

_____

POINT OF VIEW _____

FROG	TOAD
Looks Like _____	Looks Like _____
_____	_____
_____	_____
Says _____	Says _____
_____	_____
_____	_____
Does _____	Does _____
_____	_____
_____	_____
Others Say _____	Other Say _____
_____	_____
_____	_____
Author Says _____	Author Says _____
_____	_____
_____	_____

Transforming Storytimes into Reading and Writing Lessons

CHAPTER 7

Caldecott Books

Caldecott medal and honor books are excellent vehicles to teach reading objectives. They can be used to teach the skill of compare and contrast. Some titles are clear examples of literary elements. The books as a whole also represent diverse cultures as well as the best in children's literature.

▷ OBJECTIVES

The NCTE/IRA national standards, and state and local standards can be addressed through the content of Caldecott books. Objectives for NCTE/IRA Standard Three, that students use many strategies to comprehend, interpret, evaluate, and appreciate books, are included in the lessons on literary elements. Objectives for Standard Four, that students communicate orally with a variety of audiences, are included in the readers' theater and puppet show lessons.

Objectives that are tested on the Stanford Achievement Test (SAT 9) can be addressed by lessons in this chapter. Sequencing and compare and contrast are specifically targeted.

A list of Caldecott books by literary elements is included. By using the lesson plans of the last chapter on literary elements but inserting the Caldecott titles, the school library media specialist can teach literary elements using the content of Caldecott books. This addresses the SAT 9 objectives of inferences based on character, plot, and theme.

▶ COLLABORATION

Before embarking on the Caldecott unit, it is essential to have a planning meeting with all the teachers of the grade level, along with the teachers of special education classes that are participating, and the art, music, and computer lab teachers. This meeting is another word for collaboration, the underlying concept of *IP 2*. The Caldecott unit is aimed at second grade, but can be used with grades three or four. During the planning meeting, discuss the particular objectives that will be addressed in the unit. Have resources available for the teachers so they can integrate Caldecott books into their content units. Some suggestions are Shan Glandon's *Caldecott Connections to Language Arts, Caldecott Connections to Science,* and *Caldecott Connections to Social Studies,* all published by Libraries Unlimited in 2000. The library media specialist and the art teacher will find The Association for Library Services to Children's *Newbery and Caldecott Awards: A Guide to the Medal and Honor Books* (American Library Association, 2000) helpful in pinpointing methods of illustrations used in the Caldecott books.

The library media specialist provides the initial instruction about Randolph Caldecott and the medal, primary instruction on each of the objectives during storytime, small Caldecott libraries for each classroom, a Caldecott poster (available from Follett Library Resources), the scripts and puppets for the plays, final rehearsals in the library, the venue for the performances, Caldecott reading record forms, and Caldecott fan club cards for students. The recording form can be found at the end of this chapter.

> This meeting is another word for collaboration, the underlying concept of IP 2.

Teachers, in the supportive role, should be expected to read Caldecott books during their own classroom storytimes to reinforce the objectives. They are also in charge of giving students silent reading time to read the books so all students will read at least five to ten books on their own before the readers' theater or puppet show celebration. Remember to include some of the easiest to read such as *Yo! Yes?, Freight Train, The Paperboy, Time Flies, Snow, No, David!* and *Ten, Nine, Eight.* The teachers should have students record the titles they have read on the reading record the school library media specialist provides.

Teachers should provide practice time for the puppet shows, particularly the oral reading. The teachers are given options from which they can choose the puppet show or play. The library media specialist writes down each teacher's choice. The date for the puppet show celebration will be determined during this meeting. Request that the classroom teachers have the students write letters of invitation to their parents a week before the culminating activity. Announce the Caldecott Art Contest. Students may submit drawings to be used on the fan club cards. The judges of the contest are the library media specialist and the teachers involved in the project. The library media specialist provides the printed Caldecott fan club cards. The classroom teachers fill in the names of the students and give them out after the culminating activity.

Consider having refreshments. Sheet cakes can be ordered with the Caldecott emblem. Or consider serving foods from the books, such as rice cakes *(The Funny Little Woman),* bread *(The Fool of the World and the Flying Ship),* wedding cake *(Frog Went A ' Courtin'),* maple sugar candy *(The Biggest Bear),* cookies in the shape of dog bones *(Finders Keepers),* rapunzel or a leafy lettuce *(Rapunzel),* milk *(One Fine Day),* tea *(May I Bring a Friend?),* and hot chocolate *(The Polar Express).* If there are more than five classes participating, it is best to have two separate culminating activities to accommodate the students' attention spans.

Ask the art teacher to have the students experiment with the methods of Caldecott artists. Be sure to provide plenty of examples of Caldecott illustrations, along with the book *What Do Illustrators Do?* by Eileen Christelow (Clarion, 1999).

Ask the music teacher to teach the students some of the songs contained in Caldecott books: *Joseph Had a Little Overcoat* by Simms Taback (Viking, 1999), *Frog Went A' Courtin'* by John Langstaff (Harcourt Brace, 1983), *There Was an Old Woman Who Swallowed a Fly* by Simms Taback (Viking, 1997), *The Fox Went Out on a Chilly Night* by Peter Spier (Doubleday, 1961), and *One Wide River to Cross* by Barbara Emberley (Holt, 1966).

If the school has a computer lab with Internet accessibility, provide the computer teacher or assistant with the addresses of sites on the Caldecott Medal and those of Caldecott artists, along with specific ideas on how these can be used effectively. The ideas and sites are listed in the Internet lesson. This may have to be done in the library media center or the classroom, wherever there is accessibility to the Internet. If there is no student access, use the sites for source material.

▷ PUPPET SHOWS

The scripts for several successful puppet shows are included in this chapter. They are folktales on which Caldecott books are based. In keeping with the idea of active participation, all students are part of the puppet shows. The students behind the puppet stage are not responsible for saying the words the puppets utter. The sound is too muffled, and they must concentrate on manipulating the puppets. The script is read by the students who stand on either side of the stage. The teachers assign several children to each spoken part so all students can be included and the audience is more likely to be able to hear the words. It is usually best to group strong readers with weak readers, though many students do manage to memorize their parts and don't rely on their reading ability. The puppet show lessons can be used in the library if the classroom teachers are leery of puppets.

The puppet stage is a bank of shelves covered with a plain colored sheet or a length of dark cotton material. Puppets can be purchased from many vendors, including toy stores, teaching supplies, and catalog companies, such as Oriental Trading Company <www.orientaltrading.com> or Folkmanis puppets <www.folkmanis.com>. The stick puppets for *Drummer Hoff* can be cut from two paperback editions of each book and mounted on paint sticks available free at any home improvement or paint store. To achieve the explosion for *Drummer Hoff,* tape tinsel to a paint stick and quickly wave the stick up and down. No script is needed for *Drummer Hoff,* as it is a choral reading of the book.

> It is usually best to group strong readers with weak readers, though many students do manage to memorize their parts and don't rely on their reading ability.

LESSON PLAN FOR THE START OF THE CALDECOTT UNIT

REVIEW: Explain that the illustrator is the person who creates the pictures for a book.

OBJECTIVE: Students will be introduced to the art of Randolph Caldecott, his life, and the Caldecott medal using the prewriting skill of locating sources for information (SAT 9).

DIRECT WHOLE GROUP INSTRUCTION: Hold up a Caldecott Medal book that has the gold medal on it. Explain who gives the medal (librarians, the Association for Library Services to children of the American Library Association), when it is given (annually announced in January, presented in June or July at the American Library Association conference), why it is given (to an illustrator for the most distinguished picture book published in the United States the preceding year), and for whom it is named (Randolph Caldecott).

Ask the students what they would like to know about Randolph Caldecott. Jot down their suggestions. Explain all the different sources available to answer those questions and look up the answers.

- General encyclopedias—birth and death dates
- Special encyclopedias like *Something About the Author* (Gale Research)—more detailed information and photos of his illustrations
- The card or computer catalog to locate books illustrated by Caldecott and books about awards
- The official Caldecott medal official Web site: <www.ala.org/alsc/caldecott.html>

Read the students one of Randolph Caldecott's books.

REVIEW: Ask the students to chorally respond to the questions "What is the name of the medal we talked about today?" and "For what reason is it given?"

LESSON PLAN ON COMPARE AND CONTRAST

REVIEW: Explain what the words "same" and "different" mean by asking for examples of fruits. Ask the students what is the same about the fruits (seeds, come from plants). Ask them the differences (color, size, taste).

OBJECTIVE: Students will compare and contrast two Caldecott books that have been read to them (SAT 9).

DIRECT WHOLE GROUP INSTRUCTION: Explain to the students that they need to notice things that are the same and different in the stories. Read *Anansi the Spider* by Gerald McDermott (Holt, 1972) and *A Story! A Story!* by Gail Haley (Atheneum, 1970).

GUIDED STUDENT PRACTICE: Ask the students to think of three things that were the same or different in the two books read. Give think time. Use pair share.

CLOSURE: Have the students report what was the same and different. If they come up with only surface comparisons (both won the Caldecott award, both have the same main character, both have the sky god, one looks like a spider, one does not, the colors are muted in one, bright in the other), model some deeper responses:

- Both tell how something came about. *Anansi the Spider* tells why the moon is in the sky. *A Story! A Story!* tells how stories came to be.
- In *Anansi the Spider*, the sons all use their special talents to help their father. In *A Story! A Story!* Anansi uses his cleverness to perform his tasks.
- The illustrations in *A Story! A Story!* reflect the environment of the setting. *Anansi the Spider* does not reflect much of the setting.

Repeat this plan with the pairing of other Caldecott books. Some suggestions are:

- *The Funny Little Woman* by Arlene Mosel (Dutton, 1972) and *Where the Wild Things Are* by Maurice Sendak (Harper, 1963)
- *Tuesday* by David Wiesner (Clarion, 1991) and *Frog Went A' Courtin'* by John Langstaff (Harcourt, 1983)
- *Snow*, by Uri Shulevitz (Farrar, 1998), *The Snowy Day*, by Ezra Jack Keats (Puffin, 1962), *The Big Snow* by Berta and Elmer Hader (Macmillan, 1976), and *Snowflake Bentley* by Jacqueline Briggs (Houghton, 1998)
- *It Could Always Be Worse* by Margot Zemach (Farrar, 1976) and *Frederick* by Leo Lionni (Pantheon,1967)
- *Hush! A Thai Lullaby* by Minfong Ho (Orchard, 1996) and *Ten, Nine, Eight* by Molly Bang (Greenwillow, 1983)
- *Blueberries for Sal* by Robert McCloskey (Viking, 1948) and *The Biggest Bear* by Lynd Ward (Houghton Mifflin, 1952)
- *Joseph Had a Little Coat* by Sims Taback (Viking, 1999) and *Seven Blind Mice* by Ed Young (Philomel, 1972)
- *No, David!*, by David Shannon (Scholastic, 1997) and *Yo! Yes!* by Chris Raschka (Orchard, 1993)
- *May I Bring a Friend?* by Beatrice Schenk de Regniers (Atheneum, 1964) and *McElligot's Pool* by Dr. Seuss (Random, 1974)
- *Mufaro's Beautiful Daughters* by John Steptoe (Morrow, 1987) and *Cinderella* by Marcia Brown (Macmillan, 1951)

▶ CALDECOTT BOOKS AND LITERARY ELEMENTS

Use the lesson plans in the chapter on literary elements to introduce the elements or review them. After the students are proficient at discussing the literary elements, pair two Caldecott books by literary element and have the students compare them by element.

CHARACTER
Ackerman, Karen, *Song and Dance Man*. Knopf, 1988.
Bang, Molly, *When Sophie Gets Angry—Really, Really Angry*. Scholastic, 1999.
Goble, Paul, *The Girl Who Loved Wild Horses*. Bradbury, 1978.
Henkes, Kevin, *Owen*. Greenwillow, 1993.
Lionni, Leo, *Alexander and the Wind-Up Mouse*. Knopf, 1969.
Lobel, Arnold, *Frog and Toad Are Friends*. HarperCollins, 1970.
McCully, Emily Arnold, *Mirette on the High Wire*. Putnam, 1992.
Ringold, Faith, *Tar Beach*. Crown, 1991.
Williams, Vera B., *A Chair for My Mother*. Greenwillow, 1982.

SETTING

Bang, Molly, *Ten, Nine, Eight.* Greenwillow, 1983.

Bunting, Eve, *Smoky Night.* Harcourt, 1994.

Burton, Virginia Lee, *The Little House.* Houghton, 1969.

Feelings, Muriel, *Moja Means One.* Dial, 1971.

Isadora, Rachel, *Ben's Trumpet.* Greenwillow, 1979.

McCloskey, Robert, *Make Way for Ducklings.* Viking, 1969.

Shulevitz, Uri, *Snow.* Farrar, 1998

Van Allsburg, Chris, *Polar Express.* Houghton, 1985.

Wood, Audrey, *King Bidgood's in the Bathtub.* Harcourt, 1985.

Yolen, Jane, *Owl Moon.* Philomel, 1987.

PLOT (PROBLEM AND SOLUTION OR BY TYPE OF CONFLICT)

DePaola, Tomie, *Strega Nona.* Prentice-Hall, 1975.

Haley, Gail E. *A Story! A Story!* Atheneum, 1970.

Keats, Ezra Jack, *Goggles.* Macmillan, 1969.

Kimmel, Eric, *Hershel and the Hanukkah Goblins.* Holiday House, 1989.

Lester, Julius. *John Henry.* Dial, 1994.

Mosel, Arlene, *The Funny Little Woman.* Dutton, 1972.

Sendak, Maurice, *Where the Wild Things Are.* Harper, 1963.

Shannon, David, *No David!* Scholastic, 1998.

Snyder, Diane, *Boy of the Three Year Nap.* Houghton, 1988.

Steig, William, *Dr. De Soto.* Simon & Schuster, 1969.

Steig, William, *Sylvester and the Magic Pebble.* Simon & Schuster, 1969.

Wisniewski, David, *Golem.* Clarion, 1996.

Young, Ed, *Lon Po Po: A Red-Riding Hood Story from China.* Philomel, 1989.

Zelinsky, Paul O., *Rapunzel.* Dutton, 1998.

POINT OF VIEW

Birnbaum, A., *Green Eyes.* Capitol, 1953.

Lobel, Arnold, *On Market Street.* Greenwillow, 1981.

Raschka, Chris, *Yo! Yes!* Orchard, 1993.

Rylant, Cynthia, *When I Was Young in the Mountains.* Dutton, 1982.

Stewart, Sarah, *The Gardener.* Farrar, 1998.

THEME

Andersen, Hans Christian, *Ugly Duckling* (illustrated by Jerry Pinkney). Morrow, 1999.

Brown, Marcia, *Once a Mouse . . .* Scribner, 1961.

Cooney, Barbara, *Chanticleer and the Fox.* Crowell, 1958.

Lionni, Leo, *Frederick.* Pantheon, 1967.

Lionni, Leo, *Swimmy.* Pantheon, 1963.

Lobel, Arnold, *Fables.* HarperCollins, 1980.

Rathman, Peggy, *Officer Buckle and Gloria.* Putnam, 1995

Shulevitz, Uri, *The Treasure.* Farrar, 1979.

Will, *Finders Keepers.* HarcourtBrace, 1979.

Yorinks, Arthur, *Hey, Al!* Farrar, 1986.

Young, Ed, *Seven Blind Mice.* Philomel, 1992.

Zemach, Harve, *The Judge: An Untrue Tale.* Farrar, 1969.

Zemach, Margot, *It Could Always Be Worse.* Farrar, 1977.

LESSON PLAN FOR SEQUENCING

REVIEW: The plot is the series of events that happen in a story.

OBJECTIVE: Students will be able to sequence the events of a story.

DIRECT WHOLE GROUP INSTRUCTION: Read one of the books on the list below. Use the Cloze method, pausing so students fill in the expected response. When beginning to use this method, the author has found it helpful to teach students that an open palm, extended toward them, is the signal to chorally respond. After the students are familiar with the Cloze method, the pause in itself becomes the signal to chorally say the word or phrase.

- Aardema, Verna, *Why Mosquitoes Buzz in People's Ears.* Dial, 1975.
- Hogrogian, Nonny, *One Fine Day.* Macmillan, 1971.
- Low, Joseph, *Mice Twice.* McElderry/Atheneum, 1980.
- Tabach, Simms, *There Was an Old Woman.* Viking, 1997.

GUIDED STUDENT PRACTICE: Divide the group by the number of characters (including grass and water if they do an action) in each book. Give each student in a group a character. (Use two paperback versions of each book for each set of characters.) The students' task is to put in order the story's sequence of events.

CLOSURE: Have all the students repeat the story, with each student coming forward as his or her character is named.

INTERNET-BASED LESSON PLAN

PREPARATION: Assign each student an illustrator who is listed on the site and make sure they have checked out the Caldecott book by that illustrator. Search for sites by either typing the full name of the illustrator or typing in illustrators. Remember to use several search engines, such as <www.askjeeves.com> and <www.dogpile.com> to reach a variety of sites. Bookmark the sites. Following is a sampling of sites available:

<www.friend.ly.net/scoop/biographies> for Tom Feelings, Denise Fleming, Susan Jeffers, Robert Lawson, Robert McCloskey, Gerald McDermott, Jerry Pinkney, Allen Say, Janet Stevens, Don Wood, David Wisniewski, and Paul O. Zelinsky.

<www.peggyrathmann.com> for Peggy Rathman

<www.ncil.org> the National Center for Children's Illustrated Literature for Janet Stevens, Kevin Henkes, Jerry and Brian Pinkney, David Wisner, and Paul O. Zelinsky.

<www.albany.edu/museum/www.museum/bron/about-2.html> for Marcia Brown

<www.mcps.k12.md.vs/school/springbrookhs/keats.html> for Ezra Jack Keats

<www.bpib.com/illustrahtm#illustratorpage> for Leo and Diane Dillon

REVIEW: Sites on the Internet are only as reliable as the people who write them.

OBJECTIVES: 1.Students will search and find information about a Caldecott author to share with their families. 2. Families will become involved with the Caldecott unit and read a book illustrated by the person researched.

DIRECT WHOLE GROUP INSTRUCTION: Use an LCD panel, data projector, or smart board to show the students how to locate the bookmark and go to the site.

GUIDED STUDENT PRACTICE: Students find their assigned illustrator and print out the information.

CLOSURE: Have students review how and where they got their information.

HOMEWORK: Parents will read the biographical material on the assigned illustrator to their children, as well as the Caldecott book the illustrator did.
Another site to check out is <www.uta.edu/library/guides/caldecott.html>

LESSON PLAN

LESSON PLANS FOR PUPPET SHOWS

Note: That the scripts are not directly from the Caldecott books, due to copyright laws. The scripts are folk songs or folktales in the public domain. Permission was granted by the publisher of *Tops and Bottoms.*

Lesson 1

REVIEW: Reread the story on which the puppet show is based.

OBJECTIVE: Students will practice fluency and expression in oral reading.

DIRECT WHOLE GROUP INSTRUCTION: Give each student a copy of the puppet show, after having highlighted the different parts. Assign the parts, a few students to each, so all students have a part.

GUIDED STUDENT PRACTICE: Have the students read the play orally. Model the reading, if necessary.

INDEPENDENT STUDENT PRACTICE: Each group of students practices its assigned part.

CLOSURE: Have the students chorally respond to "What Caldecott book is this play based on?"

Note: If the teacher will provide the reading practice in the classroom, lesson 2 can be done about two weeks later. If the library media specialist is providing all the practice, repeat the student practice of lesson 1 until the reading is fluent.

Lesson 2

REVIEW: Name the Caldecott book on which the play is based.

OBJECTIVE: Students will adjust their spoken language to communicate with an audience. (NCTE/IRA Standard Four)

DIRECT WHOLE GROUP INSTRUCTION: Show the students the puppets, explaining which is which. Show the basic puppet moves and reiterate that the puppet should be moving in some way when the character is speaking. Choose the puppeteers. Consider choosing the most halting readers and students who do not speak English so these students can participate fully. Line up the puppeteers according to when their character will be on stage. Place the readers to the right and left of the stage, with students with the same part standing together. Stand behind the stage and direct the puppeteers while the classroom teacher directs the readers.

STUDENT PRACTICE: Do several rehearsals with the puppeteers and the readers working together.

CLOSURE: Collect the puppets and have the students chorally respond to "On which Caldecott book is this play based?"

The special education classes can either be paired with a regular education class or put on a show of their own. If these students are putting on their own show and do not read, have the teacher, the teacher's assistants, the library media specialist, or the library assistant narrate. The best choices in that instance are either to read *Where the Wild Things Are* by Maurice Sendak (Harper & Row, 1963), have the students make masks, and act out the play, or to make stick puppets of *There Was an Old Lady Who Swallowed a Fly* illustrated by Sims Taback (Viking, 1997) and have the students step forward as their animal is mentioned. A large female puppet pretends to eat the other puppets. Patterns for the animal stick puppets are readily available in flannel board storytelling books, such as Judy Sierra's *Flannel Board Storytelling Book* (H.W. Wilson, 1987), Judy Sierra's *Multicultural Folktales for the Feltboard and Readers' Theater* (Oryx, 1996), Judy Sierra and Robert Kaminski's *Multicultural Folktales: Stories to Tell Young Children* (Oryx, 1991), Doris Lynn Hicks's *Flannel Board Classic Tales* (ALA, 1997), or Paul S. Anderson's classic *Storytelling with the Flannel Board* (T.S. Dennison, 1963).

I Know an Old Lady Who Swallowed a Fly

An old English folk song

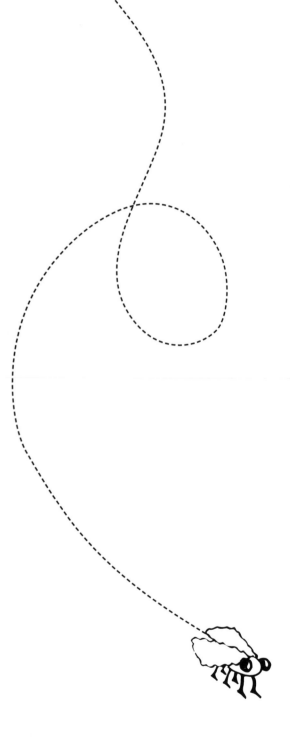

I know an old lady who swallowed a fly.
I don't know why she swallowed a fly.
Perhaps she'll die.

I know an old lady who swallowed a spider.
It wriggled and jiggled and tickled inside her.
She swallowed the spider to catch the fly.
I don't know why she swallowed a fly.
Perhaps she'll die.

I know an old lady who swallowed a bird.
How absurd! She swallowed a bird!
She swallowed the bird to catch the spider,
That wriggled and jiggled and tickled inside her.
She swallowed the spider to catch the fly.
I don't know why she swallowed a fly.
Perhaps she'll die.

I know an old lady who swallowed a cat.
Imagine that! She swallowed a cat!
She swallowed the cat to catch the bird.
She swallowed the bird to catch the spider,
That wriggled and jiggled and tickled inside her.
She swallowed the spider to catch the fly.
I don't know why she swallowed a fly.
Perhaps she'll die.

I know an old lady who swallowed a dog.
My, what a hog! She swallowed a dog!
She swallowed the dog to catch the cat.
She swallowed the cat to catch the bird.
She swallowed the bird to catch the spider,
That wriggled and jiggled and tickled inside her.
She swallowed the spider to catch the fly.
I don't know why she swallowed a fly.
Perhaps she'll die.

I know an old lady who swallowed a goat.
Just opened her throat and swallowed that goat!
She swallowed the goat to catch the dog.
She swallowed the dog to catch the cat.
She swallowed the cat to catch the bird.
She swallowed the bird to catch the spider,
That wriggled and jiggled and tickled inside her.
She swallowed the spider to catch the fly.
I don't know why she swallowed a fly.
Perhaps she'll die.

I know an old lady who swallowed a cow.
I don't know how she swallowed a cow!
She swallowed the cow to catch the goat.
She swallowed the goat to catch the dog.
She swallowed the dog to catch the cat.
She swallowed the cat to catch the bird.
She swallowed the bird to catch the spider,
That wriggled and jiggled and tickled inside her.
She swallowed the spider to catch the fly.
I don't know why she swallowed a fly.
Perhaps she'll die.

I know an old lady who swallowed a horse.
She's dead, of course!

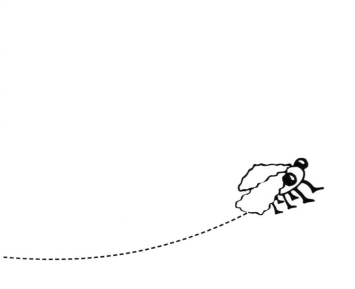

Could Anything Be Worse?

An old Jewish tale retold by Annie Weissman

CHARACTERS:

Narrators 1,2,3,4,5	Rabbi
Husband	Chickens
Wife	Rooster
Husband's Mother	Goat
Son	Cow
Daughter	Donkey

Narrator 1: Once upon a time a man lived with his wife, his mother, and his children in a tiny house.

Son: Give me back my book!

Daughter: It's not your book! It's mine!

Wife: Children, stop arguing!

Husband's Mother: Why are you yelling at the children?

Husband: I can't take it anymore. I'm going to see the rabbi.

Narrator 1: So the husband went to see the rabbi.

Husband: Rabbi! I live in a tiny house with my children, my wife, and my mother. Everyone is always screaming. Could anything be worse?

Rabbi: Hmm, let me think about this. Hmm. Do you have any chickens?

Husband: Yes, I own a few, and a rooster, too.

Rabbi: Bring them in the house to live with you.

Husband: If that will help, I'll do as you say, Rabbi.

Narrator 1: The husband went home and brought the chickens in the house.

Chickens: Cluck! Cluck! Cluck!

Rooster: Cock-a-doodle–doo! Cock-a-doodle–doo!

Wife: There are eggs everywhere! The children are smashing them under their shoes!

Husband's Mother: What a mess!

Daughter: That rooster wakes us up too early!

Son: A chicken just pecked me!

Husband: I can't stand the noise!

Narrator 2: The husband went to see the rabbi.

Husband: Rabbi! My children, my wife, and my mother are still fighting and complaining! The chickens are laying eggs everywhere, and the rooster wakes us up! Could anything be worse?

Rabbi: Hmm, let me think about this. Hmm. Do you have any goats?

Husband: One goat.

Rabbi: Good! Take it to live inside with you.

Narrator 2: So the husband went home and took the goat into the house.

Daughter: That goat is eating my clothes!

Son: Hey, don't hit me!

Daughter: It wasn't me! The goat butted you!

Wife: No eggs for breakfast! The goat stomped on them, then licked them up!

Husband's Mother: That goat is nibbling my knitting!

Goat: Naaa! Naaa!

Chickens: Cluck! Cluck! Cluck!

Rooster: Cock-a-doodle–doo! Cock-a-doodle–doo!

Husband: I can't stand the noise and confusion!

Narrator 3: So the husband went back to the rabbi.

Husband: Rabbi! My children, my wife, and my mother are still fighting and complaining! The goat is eating up our things and our food! Could anything be worse?

Rabbi: Hmm, let me think about this. Hmm. Do you have a cow?

Husband: Yes, I do, Rabbi.

Rabbi: Good! Take it to live inside with you.

Narrator 3: So the husband went home and took the cow into the house.

Cow: Moo! Moo! Moo!

Goat: Naaa! Naaa!

Chickens: Cluck! Cluck! Cluck!

Rooster: Cock-a-doodle–doo! Cock-a-doodle–doo!

Son: That cow doesn't stop mooing! I haven't slept in days!

Daughter: The cow's bell is driving me crazy!

Wife: That cow keeps tracking in mud!

Husband's Mother: That cow stomped on my foot!

Husband: I can't stand the noise and confusion!

Narrator 4: So the husband went back to the rabbi.

Husband: Rabbi! My children, my wife, and my mother are still complaining! Eggs are everywhere! I have a bruise from where the goat butted me! The cow is too upset to give any milk! Could anything be worse?

Rabbi: Hmm, let me think about this. Hmm. Do you have a donkey?

Husband: Yes, I do, Rabbi.

Rabbi: Good! Take it to live inside with you.

Husband: Are you sure about this, Rabbi? Will this help me out?

Rabbi: Don't argue with me! I know what I'm advising!

Narrator 3: So the husband went home and took the donkey into the house.

Donkey: Hee-haw! Hee-haw! Hee-haw!

Cow: Moo! Moo! Moo!

Goat: Naaa! Naaa!

Chickens: Cluck! Cluck! Cluck!

Rooster: Cock-a-doodle–doo! Cock-a-doodle–doo!

Son and daughter: The donkey keeps kicking me!

Wife: I can't get anything done because this donkey won't get out of the way!

Husband's Mother: The goat is at my knitting again!

Husband: I can't stand the noise and confusion!

Narrator 5: So the husband went back to the rabbi.

Husband: Rabbi! We have no milk! The goat chewed on my books! We can't get in the door because the donkey won't move out of the way! We get no sleep between the cock-a-doodle-doing and the mooing! Could anything be worse?

Rabbi: Hmm, let me think about this. Hmm. Do the donkey and cow have a place to live, other than your house?

Husband: Yes, Rabbi. We have a barn.

Rabbi: Then take them out to the barn. Does the goat have somewhere to live, other than your house?

Husband: Yes, Rabbi. We have a pen for it.

Rabbi: Good, then put the goat out in the pen. And the chickens? Do they have a place to live, other than your house?

Husband: Yes, Rabbi, they can live in the coop with the rooster.

Rabbi: Good, then put the rooster and the chickens in the coop.

Husband: I will, Rabbi.

Narrator 5: So the husband went home and took the donkey and the cow to the barn, the goat to its pen, and the chickens and the rooster to their coop. Then he, his wife, his mother, and his children cleaned up the tiny house. After a week, the husband went to see the rabbi.

Husband: Rabbi, how can I thank you? My life is so peaceful now! With only my wife, my mother, and my children, our house is quite big enough! And so quiet! Thank you so much, Rabbi!

Narrator 5: And so things never got worse again.

Tops and Bottoms

An African-American folktale retold by Janet Stevens
Scripted by Annie Weissman

CHARACTERS:

6 Narrators	Mrs. Hare
Bear	Hare's children
Hare	

Narrator 1: Once upon a time there lived a very lazy bear who had lots of money and lots of land. His father had been a hard worker and a smart business bear. He had given all his money and land to his son.

Bear: All I want to do is sleep.

Narrator 2: Not far down the road lived a hare. Although Hare was clever, he sometimes got into trouble.

Hare: I once owned land, too. But now I have nothing. I lost a risky bet with a tortoise and sold all of my land to Bear to pay off the debt.

Mrs. Hare: We are in very bad shape.

Hare's children: We are so hungry!

Mrs. Hare: We must think of something!

Narrator 3: So Hare and Mrs. Hare put their heads together and cooked up a plan.

The next day Hare hopped down the road to Bear's house.
Of course, Bear was asleep.

Hare: Hello, Bear! Wake up! It's your neighbor, Hare, and I have an idea.

Bear: Grunt, grunt!

Hare: We can be business partners. All we need is this field right here in front of your house. I'll do the hard work of planting and harvesting. We can split the profit right down the middle. Yes, sir, Bear. We're in this together. I'll work and you'll sleep.

Bear: Huh?

Hare: So what will it be, Bear? The top half or the bottom half? It's up to you—tops or bottoms.

Bear: Uh, let's see. I'll take the top half, Hare. Right, tops.

Hare: It's a done deal.

Narrator 3: So Bear went back to sleep, and Hare and his family went to work.

Hare: I'm planting!

Mrs. Hare: I'm watering!

Hare's children: We're weeding!

Narrator 3: Bear slept as the crops grew. Finally it was time for the harvest.

Hare: Wake up, Bear! You get the tops and I get the bottoms.

Narrator 4: Hare and his family dug up the carrots, the radishes, and the beets.

Hare: I'm plucking off the tops and tossing them into a pile for Bear. I'll keep the bottoms, all the carrots, radishes, and beets, for my family!

Bear: I'm looking at my pile, Hare, and you have all the best parts in your half!

Hare: You chose the tops, Bear.

Bear: Hare, you tricked me! You plant this field again. This season I want the bottoms!

Hare: It's a done deal, Bear.

Narrator 4: So Bear went back to sleep. Hare and his family went to work.

Hare: I'm planting!

Mrs. Hare: I'm watering!

Hare's children: We're weeding!

Narrator 4: Bear slept as the crops grew.

Hare: It's time for the harvest. Wake up, Bear! You get the bottoms and I get the tops.

Mrs. Hare: Our family is gathering the lettuce, the broccoli, and the celery.

Hare's children: We're pulling off the bottoms for Bear and putting the tops in our family's pile.

Bear: I'm looking at my pile and I am not happy! Hare, you have cheated me again.

Hare: But Bear, you wanted the bottoms this time.

Bear: Growl! You plant this field again, hare. You've tricked me twice and you owe me one season of both tops and bottoms!

Hare: You're right, poor old Bear. It's only fair that you get both tops and bottoms this time. It's a done deal, Bear.

Narrator 5: So Bear went back to sleep.

Hare: I'm planting!

Mrs. Hare: I'm watering!

Hare's children: We're weeding!

Narrator 5: Bear slept as the crops grew.

Hare: It's time for the harvest. Wake up, Bear! This time you get the tops and the bottoms.

Narrator 6: There in front of Bear's house lay a high field of corn.

Mrs. Hare: Let's yank up every cornstalk.

Hare: I'll tug off the roots at the bottoms and the tassels at the top and put them in a pile for Bear.

Hare's children: We'll collect the ears of corn in the middle and place them in our family's pile.

Hare: See, Bear. You get the tops and the bottoms. I get the middles. Yes, sir, Bear. It's a done deal!

Bear: That's it, Hare! From now on I'll plant my own crops and take the tops, the bottoms, and the middles! I'm not going to sleep through a season of planting and harvesting again!

Narrator 6: Hare and his family scooped up the corn. They hopped down the road toward home.

Hare: We can buy back our land with the profit from the crops.

Mrs. Hare: I'm going to open a vegetable stand.

Narrator 6: Hare and Bear learned to live happily as neighbors. They never were business partners again.

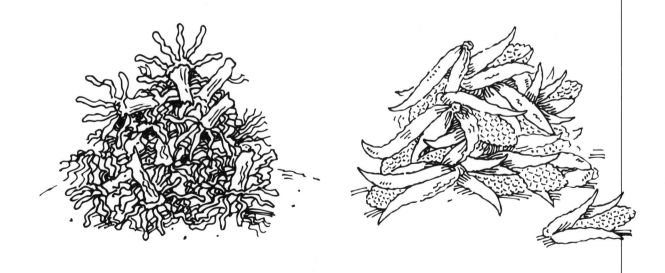

CALDECOTT READING RECORD

List the titles of Caldecott Medal and Honor Books you have read:

1. _____

2. _____

3. _____

4. _____

5. _____

6. _____

7. _____

8. _____

9. _____

10. _____

11. _____

12. _____

13. _____

14. _____

15. _____

16. _____

17. _____

18. _____

CHAPTER 8

Folktales

▶ OBJECTIVES

Folktales are the mainstay of many storytimes. With a little introduction and some carefully chosen questions, these storytimes can teach the NCTE/IRA objectives of discussing and critiquing print materials, and evaluating and synthesizing data. The objective of communicating effectively can be taught with either the flannel board or the puppet show activities. The SAT 9 objectives of elements of literature and compare and contrast are addressed in lessons in this chapter.

The information gathering activity addresses Information Literacy Standards One, Two, and Three of *IP 2:*

■ Students access information efficiently and effectively.

■ Students evaluate information critically and competently.

■ Students use information accurately and creatively.

The analysis of folktales gives students practice in problem solving and thinking behaviors. *IP 2* requires school library media specialists to plan activities like these, which involve higher level thinking skills. The writing activities included in this chapter address Information Literacy Standard Five of *IP 2,* to develop creative products.

Before beginning a folktale unit, collaborate with the teachers of the grade level, any special education teachers involved, and the art and the music teachers. These lessons are designed for third or fourth graders but can be adapted for other grade levels. The planning meeting should include an agreement on who will be responsible for which parts of the teaching and learning. The school library media specialist should provide classroom collections of folktales so teachers can share them at their read-aloud sessions. Teachers will be asked to follow the teaching pattern modeled in the library media center with respect to the thinking skills of identifying folktale elements, comparing and contrasting the stories of different countries, looking for the uniqueness of each setting, and the universality of themes and elements.

If the creative writing lessons are used, the teacher needs to complete the writing process in the classroom. The art teacher might be willing to have the students illustrate their tales in art class. Special education resource teachers will want to make the writing part of their curriculum so those students with special needs can participate fully and be proud of their products. Perhaps the music teacher will be willing to teach folk songs from around the world or folk dancing.

▶ THE ELEMENTS OF FOLKTALES

On page 34 of Archer Taylor's chapter "Folklore and the Student of Literature," from Alan Dundes's *The Study of Folklore* (Prentice Hall, 1965), Taylor gives a brief definition of folklore.

> The planning meeting should include an agreement on who will be responsible for which parts of the teaching and learning.

Folklore is the material that is handed on by tradition, either by word of mouth or by custom and practice. It may be folk songs, folktales, riddles, proverbs or other materials preserved in words. It may be traditional tools and physical objects. . . It may be traditional procedures like throwing salt over the shoulder or knocking on wood.

The elements of folklore are those things that appear over and over in most tales. The beginning of a folktale is often "once upon a time" or "long, long, ago." There is often an element of magic. The hero or heroine must perform tasks. There are special people, such as kings, queens, princes, princesses, giants, fairies, elves, wise people, witches, and wizards. There are special numbers, often 3, 7, or 12. There is repetition, often of a phrase or song. Many times there is anthropomorphism, when animals look and act like people. There are pourquoi tales about how natural things came to be. Good is rewarded and evil is punished. Sometimes the folktale points up a human foible. All of these elements are explained to the students, some during the introductory lesson, others when folktales with those elements are read or told.

INTRODUCTORY LESSON ON FOLKTALES

REVIEW: The students volunteer the titles of folktales and fairy tales they know.

OBJECTIVE: Students will be able to identify at least two elements of folktales and apply them to a story to which they have listened.

DIRECT WHOLE GROUP INSTRUCTION: Define folklore. List the elements of folktales and use an example from a well-known folktale to explain these elements.

On a globe, show where the students live: continent, country, state, and city. Read or tell a folktale from the area in which the students live.

GUIDED STUDENT PRACTICE: Ask the students to think of two folktale elements that were evident in the story. Use pair share to elicit responses.

CLOSURE: Have the students reiterate some of the elements of folktales.

AROUND THE WORLD WITH FOLKTALES LESSONS

REVIEW: Using a globe, identify the continent, country, state and city in which they live.

OBJECTIVE: Students will be able to identify at least four elements of folklore in a specific tale.

DIRECT WHOLE GROUP INSTRUCTION: Show the students how to get from their state to England, on the continent of Europe. Read or tell two of the stories from England. A list of folktales from selected countries is included in this chapter.

GUIDED STUDENT PRACTICE: Ask the students to think of specific examples of elements of folklore in these tales. After think time, use pair share for student responses.

CLOSURE: Students chorally respond to "What country did we visit?"

ADDITIONAL FOLKTALE LESSONS: Go around the world telling or reading folktales from countries, continent by continent, until you return to the United States. When visiting Africa, be sure to visit a specific country to counteract the stereotype of Africa as a single nation with a single culture. Be sure to include folktales from diverse cultures of the U.S.

COMPARE AND CONTRAST LESSON PLANS

Lesson 1

REVIEW: Ask the students to identify the geography, clothing, and plants in their environment.

OBJECTIVE: Students will compare and contrast the setting of a folktale, as gleaned from the illustrations and text, with their own environment.

DIRECT WHOLE GROUP INSTRUCTION: Read a picture book of a folktale from another country, for example, *The Fool of the World and the Flying Ship* by Arthur Ransome.

GUIDED STUDENT PRACTICE: Ask the students to look at the illustrations and find two things that are different from and two things that are the same as their environment and the setting of the story. After think time, have them do pair share. Use a whiteboard, smart board, or overhead projector to draw a Venn Diagram to visually illustrate the differences and similarities they observe.

CLOSURE: Have the students chorally "read" the Venn diagram with the library media specialist interjecting, "These are the things that are only in our setting." "These are the things that are only in the story's setting." "These are the things that are in both settings."

Venn Diagram

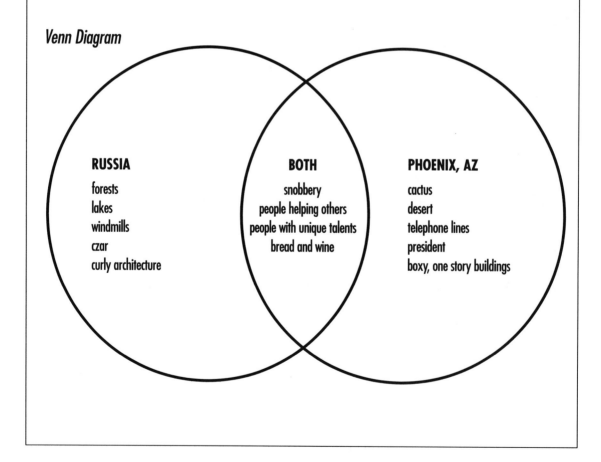

RUSSIA

forests
lakes
windmills
czar
curly architecture

BOTH

snobbery
people helping others
people with unique talents
bread and wine

PHOENIX, AZ

cactus
desert
telephone lines
president
boxy, one story buildings

Lesson 2 of Compare and Contrast

REVIEW: Have students recall some of the elements of folklore.

OBJECTIVE: Students will state the similar and disparate elements in two tales to which they have listened.

DIRECT WHOLE GROUP INSTRUCTION: Read a pair of tales from the list that follows. They are grouped by type or element.

GUIDED STUDENT PRACTICE: Ask the students to think of two things that were the same and two things that were different about the two stories. Consider using a Venn Diagram.

CLOSURE: Have students reiterate two of the more insightful things that were the same or different about the two tales.

Titles that emphasize compare and contrast

FOOLS AND TRICKSTERS

Birdseye, Tom, *Soap! Soap! Don't Forget the Soap!* Holiday House, 1993.
DePaola, Tomie, *Fin M'Coul.* Holiday House, 1981.
Goble, Paul, *Iktomi and the Buffalo Skull.* Orchard, 1991.
Hamilton, Virginia, *A Ring of Tricksters.* Blue Sky Press, 1997.
LaCapa, Michael, *The Flute Player.* Northland, 1990.
Walker, Barbara, *Just Say Hic.* Follett, 1965.
Wardlaw, Lee, *Punia and the King of the Sharks.* Dial, 1997.
Williams, Jay, *The Wicked Tricks of Tyl Uilenspiegel.* Four Winds, 1975.

POURQUOI TALES

Aardema, Verna, *Why Mosquitoes Buzz in People's Ears.* Dial, 1975.
Bruchac, Joseph and Ross, Gayle, *The Story of the Milky Way.* Dial,1995.
Duncan, Lois, *The Magic of the Spider Woman.* Scholastic, 1996.

HEROES AND HEROINES

DePaola, Tomie, *The Legend of the Indian Paintbrush.* Putnam, 1988.
Kurtz, Jane, *Miro in the Kingdom of the Sun.* Houghton Mifflin, 1996.
Sabuda, Robert, *Arthur and the Sword.* Atheneum, 1995.
San Souci, Robert D., *Brave Margaret.* Simon & Schuster, 1999.
San Souci, Robert D., *Young Arthur.* Doubleday, 1997.

Bibliography of folktales by country

ENGLAND

DeLaMare, Walter, *Molly Whuppie.* Farrar, 1983.
Galdone, Paul, *King of Cats.* Houghton, 1980.
Hodges, Margaret. *Molly Limbo.* Atheneum, 1996.
Huck, Charlotte, *Princess Furball.* Greenwillow, 1989.
Kellogg, Steven, *The Three Sillies.* Candlewick, 1999.
Kimmel, Eric, *The Old Woman and Her Pig.* Holiday House, 1992.
Robins, Arthur, *The Teeny Tiny Woman.* Candlewick, 1998.
Ross, Tony, *Lazy Jack.* Dial, 1986.
Sabuda, Robert, *Arthur and the Sword.* Atheneum, 1996.

Shulevitz, Uri, *The Treasure*. Farrar, 1978.

Wells, Rosemary, *Jack and the Beanstalk*. DK, 1997.

Williams, Marcia, *King Arthur and the Knights of the Round Table*. Candlewick, 1996.

Zemach, Harve, *Duffy and the Devil*. Farrar, 1973.

FRANCE

Bauman, Kurt, *Puss in Boots*. North-South, 1999.

Brett, Jan, *Beauty and the Beast*. Clarion, 1989.

Brown, Marcia, *Stone Soup*. Aladdin, 1997, 1947.

DeFelice, Cynthia C., *Three Perfect Peaches*. Orchard, 1995.

Ehrlich, Amy, *Cinderella*. Dial, 1985.

Huck, Charlotte S., *Toads and Diamonds*. Greenwillow, 1995.

Perrault, Charles, *Cinderella and Other Tales from Perrault*. Holt, 1989.

GERMANY

Geringer, Laura, *The Seven Ravens*. HarperCollins, 1994.

Hyman, Trina Schart, *Little Red Riding Hood*. Holiday House, 1998, 1983.

Kimmel, Eric, *Seven at One Blow: A Tale from the Brothers Grimm*. Holiday House, 1998.

Lesser, Riuka, *Hansel and Gretel*. Dutton, 1999.

Lippert, Meg, *Finest the Falcon*. Troll, 1996.

McDermott, Dennis, *The Golden Goose*. Morrow, 2000.

Ormerod, Jan, *The Frog Prince*. Lothrop, 1990.

Ray, Jane, *The Twelve Dancing Princesses*. Dutton, 1999.

Stevens, Janet, *The Bremen Town Musicians*. Holiday House, 1992.

Zelinsky, Paul O., *Rapunzel*. Dutton, 1997.

Zelinsky, Paul O., *Rumpelstilskin*. Dutton, 1986.

RUSSIA

Cole, Joanna, *Bony-Legs*. Four Winds, 1986.

Davis, Aubrey, *The Enormous Potato*. Kids Can, 1998.

Ginsburg, Mirra, *Clay Boy*. Greenwillow, 1997.

Kimmel, Eric A., *I-Know-Not-What, I-Know-Not-Where*. Holiday House, 1994.

Lurie, Alison, *The Black Geese: A Baba Yaga Tale from Russia*. DK, 1999.

McCaughrean, Geraldine, *Grandma Chickenlegs*. Carolrhoda, 1999.

Peck, Jan, *The Giant Carrot*. Dial, 1998.

Rafe, Martin, *The Language of Birds*. Putnam, 2000.

Ransome, Arthur, *The Fool of the World and the Flying Ship*. Farrar, 1987.

SanSouci, Robert D. *Peter and the Blue Witch Baby*. Doubleday, 2000.

Ziefert, Harriet, *The Snow Child*. Puffin, 2000.

JAPAN

Compton, Patricia A., *The Terrible Eek*. Simon & Schuster, 1991.

Hamanaka, Sheila, *Screen of Frogs*. Orchard, 1993.

Minarik, Rosemary, "Three Strong Women" from *Womenfolk and Fairy Tales*. Houghton Mifflin, 1975.

Mosel, Arlene, *The Funny Little Woman*. Dutton, 1972.

San Souci, Robert D., *The Samurai's Daughter*. Puffin, 1997.

Snyder, Diane, *The Boy of the Three Year Nap*. Houghton, 1988.

TRANSFORMING STORYTIMES INTO READING AND WRITING LESSONS

CHINA

Chang, Margaret Scrojin, *Da Wei's Treasure*. Margaret K. Elderberry, 1999.

Demi, *Liang and the Magic Paintbrush*. Holt, 1980.

Mosel, Arlene. *Tikki Tikki Tembo*. Dutton, 1968.

San Souci, Robert D., *Fa Mulan*. Hyperion, 1998.

Yep, Laurence, *The Boy Who Swallowed Snakes*. Scholastic, 1994.

Young, Ed, *Lon Po-Po: A Red Riding Story from China*. Philomel, 1989.

Young, Ed, *The Terrible Nung Gwama*. Collins & World, 1976.

INDIA

Brown, Marcia, *Once a Mouse . . .* Scribner, 1961.

"The Crab and the Jaguar" (text and flannel board figures included in this chapter)

Demi, *A Grain of Rice*. Scholastic, 1997.

Duff, Maggie, *Rum Pum Pum*. Macmillan, 1978.

Galdone, Paul, *The Monkey and the Crocodile*. Seabury, 1969.

IRAN

Cohen, Barbara, *Seven Daughters & Seven Sons*. Atheneum, 1982.

Kherdian, David, *The Smile of the Rose*. Holt, 1997.

Kimmel, Eric A., *Ali Baba and the Forty Thieves*. Holiday House, 1996.

TURKEY

Sierra, Judy, "Eat, Coat, Eat!" from *Multicultural Folktales for the Feltboard and Readers' Theater*. Oryx, 1996.

Walker, Barbara, *Just Say Hic*. Follett, 1965.

ISRAEL (Jewish folktales, not necessarily set in Israel)

Freedman, Florence B., *Brothers*. Harper & Row, 1985.

Gilman, Phoebe, *Something from Nothing*. Scholastic, 1992.

Hirsch, Marilyn, *The Rabbi and the Twenty-Nine Witches*. Holiday House, 1976.

Kimmel, Eric A., *Onions and Garlic*. Holiday House, 1996.

Wisniewski, David, *The Golem*. Clarion, 1996.

Zemach, Margot, *It Could Always Be Worse*. Farrar, 1990, 1976.

GHANA

Chocolate, Deborah M., *Talk! Talk!* Troll, 1993.

Kimmel, Eric, *Anansi and the Moss-Covered Rock*. Holiday House, 1988.

Lake, Mary, *The Royal Drum*. Mondo, 1996.

McDermott, Gerald, *Anansi the Spider*. Holt, 1972.

Mollel, Tolowa M., *Ananse's Feast*. Clarion, 1997.

MEXICO

Aardema, Verna, *Borreguita and the Coyote*. Random, 1981.

Ada, Alma Flor, *The Lizard in the Sun=La lagartija y el Sol*. Doubleday, 1997.

Ehlert, Lois, Cuckoo: *A Mexican Tale=Cucu: un Cuento Folklorico Mexicana*. Harcourt Brace, 1997.

Johnston, Tony, *The Tale of Rabbit and Coyote*. Putnam, 1994.

Lyons, Grant, "The Marvelous Chirionerra" from *Tales the People Tell in Mexico*. Messner, 1972.

Sauvageau, Juan, "The Ungrateful Snake" from *Tales That Must Not Die*
Volume I. Oasis, 1984.

Weissman, Anne, *The Castle of Chuchurumbel / El Castillo de Chuchurumbel.* Hispanic
Books Distributors, 1987. (Text and flannel board figures included in this chapter)

UNITED STATES

Chase, Richard, "Soap! Soap! Soap!" from *The Grandfather Tales.* Houghton Mifflin, 1948.

Courlander, Harold, "The Beetle's Hairpiece" from *People of the Short Blue Corn.*
Harcourt, 1970.

Davis, Aubrey, *Sody Sallyratus.* Kids Can, 1998.

Hayes, Joe, *The Day It Snowed Tortillas.* Mariposa, 1985.

Hayes, Joe, *Soft Child: How the Rattlesnake Got Its Fangs.* Harbinger, 1993.

Lester, Julius, "Why Dogs Hate Cats" from *The Knee-High Man and Other Tales.*
Dial, 1972.

Sloat, Terri, *Sody Sallyratus.* Dutton, 1997.

INFORMATION GATHERING LESSON PLANS

Lesson 1

Note: Before the lesson, the classroom teacher has each student pick a country from a list of the countries visited, provided by the library media specialist.

REVIEW: Review the countries that were visited during the folktale unit.

OBJECTIVE: Students will gather specific facts about a country and compare the data.

DIRECT WHOLE GROUP INSTRUCTION: The students are divided into groups, one group for each country the class visited on their "folktale" journey. Using primary encyclopedias or *The World Almanac for Kids* (World Almanac, 2000), have the students look up the population and area of the countries, after you explain what these terms mean. The students record their data on the worksheet (a copy is included in this chapter). The school library media specialist and the classroom teacher monitor and assist groups as they gather the data.

Each group reports the population data. The classroom teacher goes to each group and helps them read the large number while the school library media specialist records it on a chart, included after this lesson plan, on the overhead projector. After think time, students chorally answer which country has the most people, which has the least, and which have almost the same amount.

This is repeated for the area by square miles. The library media specialist and the students interpret the data. Which countries are crowded? Which are sparsely populated?

Data are collected in the same way for the first two farm products and the first two manufactured products. These can be shared orally. Students (and adults) may be surprised at the similarities and differences.

CLOSURE: Students review what kind of information they found and where they found it.

Lesson 2

REVIEW: Have the students review a few of their facts about the countries they are researching.

OBJECTIVE: Students will take notes, using key words, on two facts about the people of the country they are researching.

DIRECT WHOLE GROUP INSTRUCTION: Read a paragraph, which is shown on the overhead projector, about the people of one of the countries not chosen. Then have the students read the first sentence with you and decide if there are any key words. Underline the key words. Repeat for each sentence. Transfer the key words to the appropriate part of their worksheet.

INDEPENDENT PRACTICE: The students read a paragraph on the people in the country they chose and write down the key words.

DIRECT WHOLE GROUP INSTRUCTION: Use the key words the students found in the initial instruction. Using pair share, have the students compose a sentence based on those key words.

INDEPENDENT PRACTICE: Students write two sentences from the key words on the country they chose.

CLOSURE: The students read their paragraphs to a partner.

Lesson 3: The most current information using the Internet

Note: Before this lesson, bookmark sites like: <www.oanda.com> or <www.xe.net/currency>.

REVIEW: Ask the students which sources were used for researching the first two lessons. Find the copyright date of the material.

ANTICIPATORY SET: Show some real foreign currency and an American dollar.

OBJECTIVE: Students will use the Internet to find the latest information on currency in the country they are researching and how much the currency is worth in United States dollars.

DIRECT WHOLE GROUP INSTRUCTION: Using an LCD projector, data projector, or smart board, show the students how to use the bookmarked site to find out the name of the currency in their country and how much it is worth in United States dollars. Use a country the students have not picked as an example. Compare this with the information that was found in the other source (*World Almanac for Kids* or a primary encyclopedia). Point out the date of the site's information and the date of the other source used.

GUIDED STUDENT PRACTICE: Students go to the bookmarked site of their country and write down the name of the currency in their country and how much it is worth in United States dollars, and compare that with the information from the other source. The teacher and the library media specialist (or computer teacher) monitor and assist.

CLOSURE: Students share the name of the currency and its worth in United States dollars.

Note: Suggest that the classroom teacher do a lesson on graphing using the information from these lessons.

COUNTRY	POPULATION	AREA

COUNTRY	CURRENCY	WORTH IN U.S. DOLLARS

TRANSFORMING STORYTIMES INTO READING AND WRITING LESSONS

➤ FLANNEL BOARD STORYTELLING BY STUDENTS

As the folktales for the various countries are selected, think in terms of which would be candidates to tell use using a flannel board. When selecting folktales, consider repetition, stories with more than two characters, and simplicity of the story. Choose tales to represent diverse cultures. Make a black and white master of the characters, by asking the art teacher to collaborate, asking a talented student, or tracing the patterns from a book listed in the bibliography. The stories and flannel board outlines for "The Crab and the Jaguar" (India) and "The Castle of Chuchurumbel / el Castillo de Chuchurumbel" (Mexico) are included in this chapter. Copy the master and color it in using markers, watercolors, or colored pencils. Use felt tape on the back of the characters and store them in a resealable plastic bag. As a country is visited, these stories are told using the flannel board. After the tour around the world is over, tell all of the flannel board stories in one session. As the stories are told, record them on a cassette tape and duplicate it for each classroom involved in the unit. As the flannel board stories are modeled, point out "hints" on how to make and present them:

- Look at the audience, not the flannel board.
- When the teller wants the audience to participate, signal it by pausing.
- When telling a repetitive tale, like *The Castle of Chuchurumbel*, have the audience participate halfway through the story.
- Number the characters on the back in order to keep the story in the correct sequence.

Students may seek out their own tales and make their own characters, but the selection must be cleared with the library media specialist so stories that are too long or complicated are not attempted. The school library media specialist supplies the felt tape out of her budget, bought from a teaching supply company. The classroom teacher supplies the large resealable plastic bags.

The classroom teacher tallies how many copies of each story and characters are needed and copies them. The students color, cut, and affix the felt tape. The stories can be practiced either in the classroom or in the library. The management of the practices and final presentation, and the making of the flannel boards are covered in Chapter Four.

➤ PUPPET SHOWS AND READERS' THEATER

The scripts for several folktales are included at the end of this chapter. These can be used either for readers' theater or puppet shows. The lesson plans for these are in Chapter Seven, as are the scripts for the tales of *Could Anything Be Worse?* and *Tops and Bottoms*.

➤ BOOKS WITH PLAYS OR ACTIVITIES

Anderson, Dee, *Amazingly Easy Puppet Plays*. American Library Association, 1997, 235pp.

Barchers, Suzanne I., *Multicultural Folktales: Readers Theatre for Elementary Students*. Libraries Unlimited, 2000, 188pp.

Gerke, Pamela, *Multicultural Plays For Children Volume 1: Grades K–3*. Smith and Kraus, 1999, 161pp.

Gerke, Pamela, *Multicultural Plays For Children Volume 2: Grades 4–6*. Smith and Kraus, 1999, 199pp.

McCullough, L. E., *Plays from Fairy Tales*. Smith and Kraus, 1997, 183pp.

Milford, Susan, *Tales Alive! Ten Multicultural Folktales with Activities*. Williamson, 1995, 127pp.

Sierra, Judy, *The Flannel Board Storytelling Book*. H.W. Wilson, 1997, 204pp.

Sierra, Judy, *Multicultural Folktales for the Feltboard and Readers' Theater*. Oryx, 1996, 186pp.

The Castle of Chuchurumbel

Retold by Annie Weissman
Illustrated by Susan Bailyn

These are the doors
of the Castle of Chuchurumbel.

These are the keys
that opened the doors
of the Castle of Chuchurumbel.

This is the the cord
that held the keys
that opened the doors
of the Castle of Chuchurumbel.

This is the rat
that chewed the cord
that held the keys
that opened the doors
of the Castle of Chuchurumbel.

This is the cat
that ate the rat
that chewed the cord
that held the keys
that opened the doors
of the Castle of Chuchurumbel.

This is the dog
that chased the cat
that ate the rat
that chewed the cord
that held the keys
that opened the doors
of the Castle of Chuchurumbel.

This is the stick
that hit the dog
that chased the cat
that ate the rat
that chewed the cord
that held the keys
that opened the doors
of the Castle of Chuchurumbel.

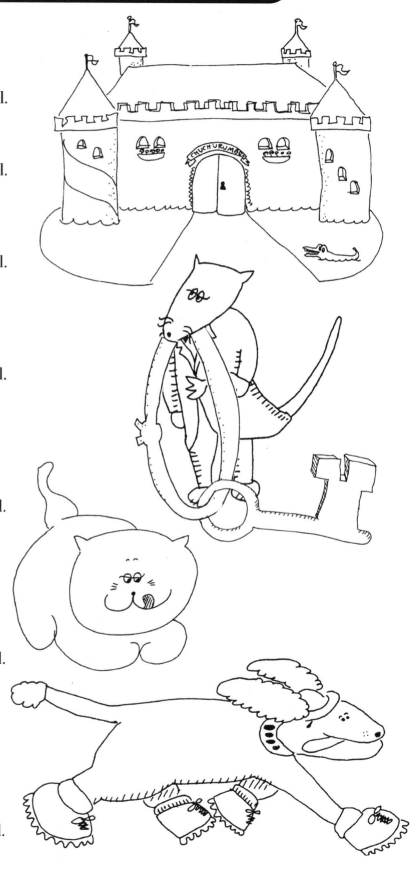

This is the fire
that burned the stick
that hit the dog
that chased the cat
that ate the rat
that chewed the cord
that held the keys
that opened the doors
of the Castle of Chuchurumbel.

This is the water
that put out the fire
that burned the stick
that hit the dog
that chased the cat
that ate the rat
that chewed the cord
that held the keys
that opened the doors
of the Castle of Chuchurumbel.

This is the ox
that drank the water
that put out the fire
that burned the stick
that hit the dog
that chased the cat
that ate the rat
that chewed the cord
that held the keys
that opened the doors
of the Castle of Chuchurumbel.

These are the people
of the Castle of Chuchurumbel
who own the ox
that drank the water
that put out the fire
that burned the stick
that hit the dog
that chased the cat
that ate the rat
that chewed the cord
that held the keys
that opened the doors
of the Castle of Chuchurumbel.

El Castillo de Chuchurumbel

Adaptado por Annie Weissman
Ilustrado por Susan Bailyn

Este es el Castillo de Chuchurumbel.

Estas son las puertas
del Castillo de Chuchurumbel.

Estas son las llaves
de las puertas
del Castillo de Chuchurumbel.

Este es el cordón
de las llaves
de las puertas
del Castillo de Chuchurumbel.

Este es el ratón
que royó el cordón
de las llaves
de las puertas
del Castillo de Chuchurumbel.

Este es el gato
que comió al ratón
que royó el cordón
de las llaves
de las puertas
del Castillo de Chuchurumbel.

Este es el perro
que correteó al gato
que comió al ratón
que royó el cordón
de las llaves
de las puertas
del Castillo de Chuchurumbel.

Este es el palo
que le pegó al perro
que correteó al gato
que comió al ratón
que royó el cordón
de las llaves
de las puertas
del Castillo de Chuchurumbel.

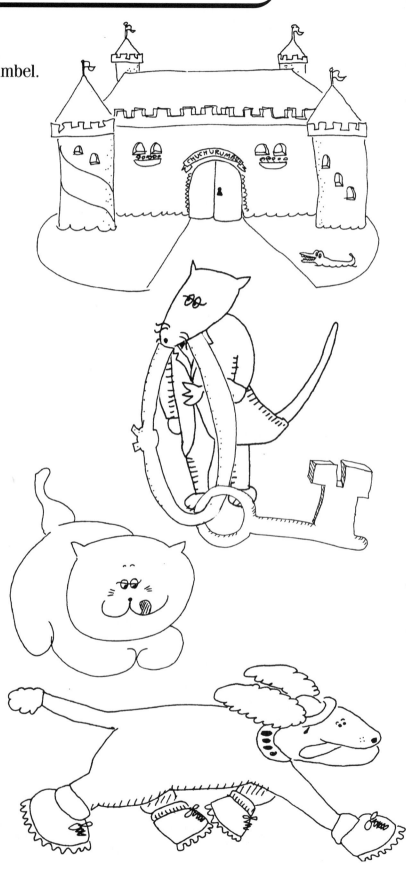

TRANSFORMING STORYTIMES INTO READING AND WRITING LESSONS

Este es el fuego
que quemó al palo
que le pegó al perro
que correteó al gato
que comió al ratón
que royó el cordón
de las llaves
de las puertas
del Castillo de Chuchurumbel.

Este es el agua
que apagó el fuego
que quemó al palo
que le pegó al perro
que correteó al gato
que comió al ratón
que royó el cordón
de las llaves
de las puertas
del Castillo de Chuchurumbel.

Este es el buey
que se bebió el agua
que apagó el fuego
que quemó al palo
que le pegó al perro
que correteó al gato
que comió al ratón
que royó el cordón
de las llaves
de las puertas
del Castillo de Chuchurumbel.

Esta es la gente del Castillo de Chuchurumbel
que son los dueños del buey
que se bebió el agua
que apagó el fuego
que quemó al palo
que le pegó al perro
que correteó al gato
que comió al ratón
que royó el cordón
de las llaves
de las puertas
del Castillo de Chuchurumbel.

The Crab and the Jaguar, A folktale from India

Adapted by Annie Weissman

Once upon a time a crab lived by the sea. He would get very bored. He used to play a game with his eyes.

"Eyes, little eyes of mine, run away to the deep blue sea. Quick, quick, quick, quick, quick!"

And his eyes would leap out of their sockets and run away to the deep blue sea.

Then the crab would say, "Eyes, little eyes of mine, come back here from the deep blue sea, quick, quick, quick, quick, quick!"

The eyes went right back into his face.

One day Mr. Jaguar was walking by when he saw Mr. Crab playing the game with his eyes.

Mr. Jaguar said, "Oh, Mr. Crab, that looks like a terrific game. Would you play that game with my eyes?"

Mr. Crab said, " I'm sorry, I can't. The terrible Animale Padole, the father of the trehira fish, lives in the deep blue sea. If I send your eyes out there, he may swim by and eat up your eyes."

"But that didn't happen with your eyes," said Mr. Jaguar.

"I know," said Mr. Crab, "but I'm willing to take a chance with my own eyes, not someone else's eyes."

"Please!" asked Mr. Jaguar.

"No!" said Mr. Crab.

"Please!"

"No!"

Mr. Jaguar begged, "Please, please, please, please, please, please!"

"All right!" said Mr. Crab. "Eyes, eyes of Mr. Jaguar, run away to the deep blue sea, quick, quick, quick, quick, quick!"

The jaguar's eyes leaped out of their sockets and ran away to the deep blue sea. In a little while the crab called the eyes back.

"Eyes, eyes of Mr. Jaguar, come back here from the deep blue sea, quick, quick, quick, quick, quick!"

The eyes went back into the jaguar's face.

"Ooh, that was fun!" said Mr. Jaguar. "Do it again! Do it again!"

"I told you I can't," said Mr. Crab. "The terrible Animale Padole, the father of the trehira fish, lives in the deep blue sea. If I send your eyes out there, he may swim by and eat up your eyes."

"But he didn't do it, did he?" said Mr. Jaguar.

"Maybe not this time, but possibly the next time," said Mr. Crab.

"I'm willing to take the risk," said Mr. Jaguar. "Do it again! Do it again!"

"No!" said Mr. Crab.

"Please!" said Mr. Jaguar.

"No!"

"Please!"

"No!"

"Please, please, please, please, please, please!"

"All right!" said Mr. Crab. "Eyes, eyes of Mr. Jaguar, run away to the deep blue sea, quick, quick, quick, quick, quick!"

The jaguar's eyes leaped out of their sockets and ran away to the deep blue sea. Right to where the Animale Padole, the father of the trehira fish, was swimming. He ate the jaguar's eyes.

Mr. Crab called, "Eyes, eyes of Mr. Jaguar, come back here from the deep blue sea, quick, quick, quick, quick, quick!"

Nothing happened.

Mr. Crab called again, "Eyes, eyes of Mr. Jaguar, come back here from the deep blue sea, quick, quick, quick, quick, quick!"

Nothing happened. The crab called many times, but the jaguar's eyes did not come back.

Mr. Crab buried himself in the sand.

Mr. Jaguar finally realized that his eyes had been eaten by the Animale Padole. He wandered along the beach until he bumped into Mr. King-Vulture.

Mr. King-Vulture said, "Say, watch where you're going!"

"I can't!" said Mr. Jaguar. "Mr. Crab sent my eyes out to the sea and the terrible Animale Padole, the father of the trahira fish, ate them up. Say, you come across a lot of eyes on animal carcasses. Could you get me another pair of eyes?"

"Why should I?" asked Mr. King-Vulture.

"If you find me new eyes, whenever I kill something for my dinner, I'll leave some for you."

So the vulture flew off and found another pair of eyes for the jaguar. He brought them back. Mr. Jaguar popped them in place.

"These new eyes are even better than the old pair!" said Mr. Jaguar.

And that's why whenever a jaguar kills something for food, it always leaves some for the vultures.

TRANSFORMING STORYTIMES INTO READING AND WRITING LESSONS

The Crab and the Jaguar, a folktale from India

Adapted and scripted by Annie Weissman

Characters:

Narrator 1	Mr. Crab
Narrator 2	Mr. Jaguar
Narrator 3	Animale Podole
Narrator 4	Mr. King–Vulture

Narrator 1: Once upon a time a crab lived by the sea. He would get very bored. He used to play a game with his eyes.

Mr. Crab: Eyes, little eyes of mine, run away to the deep blue sea. Quick, quick, quick, quick, quick!

Narrator 1: And his eyes would leap out of their sockets and run away to the deep blue sea.

Mr. Crab: Eyes, little eyes of mine, come back here from the deep blue sea, quick, quick, quick, quick, quick!

Narrator 1: And the eyes would go right back into his face. One day Mr. Jaguar was walking by when he saw Mr. Crab playing the game with his eyes.

Mr. Jaguar: Oh, Mr. Crab, that looks like a terrific game. Would you play that game with my eyes?

Mr. Crab: I'm sorry, I can't. The terrible Animale Padole, the father of the trehira fish, lives in the deep blue sea. If I send your eyes out there, he may swim by and eat up your eyes.

Mr. Jaguar: But that didn't happen with your eyes.

Mr. Crab: I know, but I'm willing to take a chance with my own eyes, not someone else's eyes.

Mr. Jaguar: Please!

Mr. Crab: No!

Mr. Jaguar: Please!

Mr. Crab: No!

Mr. Jaguar: Please, please, please, please ,please, please!

Mr. Crab: All right! Eyes, eyes of Mr. Jaguar, run away to the deep blue sea, quick, quick, quick, quick, quick!

Narrator 2: The jaguar's eyes leaped out of their sockets and ran away to the deep blue sea. In a little while the crab called the eyes back.

Mr. Crab: Eyes, eyes of Mr. Jaguar, come back here from the deep blue sea, quick, quick, quick, quick, quick!

Narrator 2: And the eyes went back into the jaguar's face.

Mr. Jaguar: Ooh, that was fun! Do it again! Do it again!

Mr. Crab: I told you, I can't. The terrible Animale Padole, the father of the trehira fish, lives in the deep blue sea. If I send your eyes out there, he may swim by and eat up your eyes.

Mr. Jaguar: But he didn't do it, did he?

Mr. Crab: Maybe not this time, but possibly the next time.

Mr. Jaguar: I'm willing to take the risk. Do it again! Do it again!

Mr. Crab: No.

Mr. Jaguar: Please!

Mr. Crab: No!

Mr. Jaguar: Please!

Mr. Crab: No!

Mr. Jaguar: Please, please, please, please, please, please!

Mr. Crab: All right! Eyes, eyes of Mr. Jaguar, run away to the deep blue sea, quick, quick, quick, quick, quick!

Narrator 2: The jaguar's eyes leaped out of their sockets and ran away to the deep blue sea. Right to where the Animale Padole, the father of the trehira fish, was swimming.

Animale Padole: Oh, yum, two eyes! Gulp!

Mr. Crab: Eyes, eyes of Mr. Jaguar, come back here from the deep blue sea, quick, quick, quick, quick, quick!

Narrator 3: Nothing happened.

Mr. Crab: Eyes, eyes of Mr. Jaguar, come back here from the deep blue sea, quick, quick, quick, quick, quick!

Narrator 3: Nothing happened. The crab called many times but the jaguar's eyes did not come back.

Mr. Crab: I'd better bury myself in the sand.

Mr. Jaguar: Hey, where are my eyes? Where are you, Mr. Crab?

Narrator 3: Finally Mr. Jaguar realized that his eyes had been eaten by the Animale Padole. He wandered along the beach until he bumped into Mr. King-Vulture.

Mr. King-Vulture: Say, watch where you're going!

Mr. Jaguar: I can't! Mr. Crab sent my eyes out to the sea and the terrible Animale Padole, the father of the trahira fish, ate them up. Say, you come across a lot of eyes on animal carcasses. Could you get me another pair of eyes?

Mr. King-Vulture: Why should I?

Mr. Jaguar: If you find me new eyes, whenever I kill something for my dinner, I'll leave some for you.

Narrator 4: So the vulture flew off and found another pair of eyes for the jaguar.

Mr. Jaguar: These new eyes are even better than the old pair!

Narrator 4: And that's why whenever a jaguar kills something for food, it always leaves some for the vultures.

The Clever Turtle, a Tale from Brazil

Adapted by Annie Weissman

CHARACTERS:

Narrator 1	Father
Narrator 2	Mother
Narrator 3	Child 1
Turtle	Child 2
Monkey	Child 3
Snake	

Narrator 1: Along the great Amazon River in Brazil, the Indians tell this tale. In the jungle forest, where all manner of plants and animals make their world, Turtle sat in her little house playing her flute. Her song was clear and sweet.

Turtle: Fing-filoo-fong, fing-filoo-fong, fing-filoo-fong, fing-filoo-fong!

Monkey: I like your song, Turtle! It has such high notes, low notes and middle notes.

Snake: I love your song, Turtle! It is a fine song!

Turtle: Thank you. I like it too.

Narrator 1: An Indian was on his way home when he heard Turtle's song.

Father: What is that sound? It is my own stomach grumbling. That turtle I see will make a fine meal. I'll catch it, take it home, and cook it. Its good meat will make my stomach quiet.

Narrator 1: He went over to Turtle's house.

Father: Turtle! Turtle! Come out! I want to see the flute on which you're playing such fine music.

Narrator 1: The music stopped.

Turtle: Uh-hoo. . . errr

Narrator 1: The father waited a little while, but Turtle did not come out.

Father: Come out, Turtle! Come out so I can see you and your flute that plays such nice music.

(Turtle comes out with the flute)

Turtle: Here I am. Here I am. You didn't have to shout so loudly. I heard you. You may see my flute.

Narrator 2: Turtle put out her flute for the Indian to see, but he grabbed Turtle by the neck and began to run through the woods to his hut.

All: Pit-i-pat, pit-i-pat, pit-i-pat.

Narrator 2: Turtle tried to cry out, but couldn't make a sound. So she closed her eyes and held her flute close to her side. When the Indian reached his hut with Turtle, his wife and children came out to meet him.

Father: I brought home Turtle! We'll cook her tomorrow and have a fine meal. I'm putting her in a cage made of branches and closing the lid. I'm putting a heavy piece of wood on top.

Mother: It's time to go to sleep.

Narrator 2: The next morning the whole family was up early.

Father: I'm going to the fields to hoe and plant. When the sun begins to go down, I'll come back and we'll cook Turtle. Whatever you do, DON'T let Turtle out of the cage!

Narrator 2: So the father went away and the children played near the hut.

Turtle: I'm thinking about what the Indian said. I think I'll play my flute. Fing-filoo-fong, fing-filoo-fong, fing-filoo-fong.

Child 1: Is that you playing, Turtle?

Turtle: Yes, I'm playing my flute. Listen! Fing-filoo-fong, fing-filoo-fong, fing-filoo-fong. I can dance, as well.

Child 2: Can you really dance?

Turtle: I can play and dance at the same time. Would you like to see that?

Child 3: Yes, we'd love to!

Turtle: It's easy. Just open this cage, and I'll show you how I dance and play at the same time. Just open the lid and watch me.

Child 1: I'll take the log off the lid.

Turtle: (Dancing) Fing-filoo-fong, fing-filoo-fong, fing-filoo- fong.

All: Thump-crush, thump-crush, thump-crush!

Child 2: Turtle looks so funny!

Turtle: Would you like to see me dance and play again?

Child 3: Oh yes, please!

Child 1 and 2: Yes! Do it again!

Turtle: Well, then, you must take me out. It's not easy to dance in this little box. My legs are stiff. Just take me out and let me take a little walk to stretch my legs. Then I'll be right back to dance and play for you again.

Child 3: We'll let you out because you played and danced so well.

Child 1: But come back quickly.

Child 2: Don't run away.

Turtle: You wait right here for me until I come back.

(They let Turtle out of the cage. Turtle crawls around and around, further away, until she disappears.)

Child 3: We are waiting a long time.

Child 1: We'd better see where that turtle is!

Child 1, 2, and 3: Turtle! Turtle!

Narrator 3: They looked everywhere, but they couldn't find her.

Child 1: I'm scared. What will we tell our father?

Child 2: Let's take a stone and paint it to look like a turtle and put it in the cage. Our father will think it's Turtle, and maybe he won't be angry with us.

(Children put a painted stone in the cage.)

Father: I'm home! Now I'll put water on the fire, and when it steams we'll put Turtle in and cook her. And when she's well cooked, we'll take off her shell and eat the tender meat.

Narrator 3: The water boiled and the father put in the painted stone.

Father: It should be ready now. Bring the earthen plate so we can eat.

Narrator 3: The children were scared, but they brought the plate. The father took out the painted stone and threw it on the plate, which broke into many pieces.

Father: You let Turtle run away!

Child 2: Yes, we did.

Child 3: We shouldn't have done it.

Child 1: What we did was wrong.

Father: I'm not angry. I understand that Turtle tricked you. I'll go and see if I can catch Turtle again. But this time, don't you let her run away.

Child 1, 2, and 3: We won't.

Father: Turtle! Turtle!

Narrator 3: Turtle was hidden deep down in her house.

Father: I'm tired. I'll catch Turtle tomorrow.

Narrator 3: Did tomorrow ever come? What do you think?

CHAPTER 9

Genre

▶ OBJECTIVES

A genre is a type of literature that shares the same elements. Using storytimes to introduce genre is one way to broaden students' reading interests by acquainting them with many different types of books. The teaching of genre pertains directly to the NCTE/IRA national Standard Two, that students read a wide range of genre.

Another reason for teaching genre is to help students write better stories of each genre, which relates to the NCTE/IRA Standard Five that students use a wide range of strategies and use different writing elements correctly for a variety of audiences. Once students understand the structure of a mystery or the essence of science fiction it will be easier for them to branch out and write these different forms. This chapter contains a sampling of genre. This unit was used with fifth graders, but could be adapted for third to twelfth grades.

▶ COLLABORATION

Before beginning a genre unit, collaborate with the classroom teacher and define the unit objectives, forms to be taught, reinforcement lessons, whether writing will be included, and the division of responsibilities between the library media specialist and the classroom teacher. It is recommended that the classroom teacher use recommended titles to reinforce the concepts and do the bulk of the writing and editing of the stories. Although six genres are included in this chapter, it would be a task to teach all of them. The library media specialist and the teacher should choose one, two, or three genres that they like (enthusiasm is catching) and that lend themselves to integration into other parts of the curriculum. If the students are researching animals, certainly animal realism and fantasy would be an obvious choice. If the students are studying a particular time in history, then historical fiction would be appropriate.

The bibliographies under each genre are short and include favorites. For a more complete listing of genre novels, see *Junior Genreflecting* by Bridget Dealy Volz, Cheryl Perkins Scheer, and Lynda Blackburn Welborn (Libraries Unlimited, 2000).

▶ MYSTERY

The study of mysteries is an excellent vehicle for ensuring that students understand that all stories must have a beginning, a middle, and an end. Gillian Roberts makes a point of this in *You Can Write a Mystery* (Writer's Digest, 1999). The crime is the beginning, the search for the answer is the middle, and the solution is the end. The conflict comes from the unsolved crime and the search for justice.

Gillian Roberts also writes that a good mystery cannot withhold necessary information from the reader. The reader must know what the detective knows. The characters and plot cannot be manipulated to fit the solution. It all must be logical.

Dean R. Koontz, in *Writing Popular Fiction* (Writers Digest, 1972), lists many requirements for mysteries. The ones that most apply to students include an appearance of the investigator at the beginning of the story, a reason to want to find the solution for the crime, and an introduction of at least two suspects in the first three chapters of a mystery.

LESSON PLAN

MYSTERY LESSON 1: IDENTIFYING THE PARTS OF A MYSTERY

REVIEW: Ask the students if anyone has recently read or seen a mystery.

OBJECTIVE: Students will identify the beginning (the crime), the middle (the search for clues and information), and the ending (the solution).

DIRECT WHOLE GROUP INSTRUCTION: Explain the objective and give an example from a school-related imaginary "crime." An example might be that an item is missing from the library, such as the pet snake or the large cut-out of Michael Jordan. The detective investigates and searches for motives and information. The detective solves the "crime." Read *Grandpa's Teeth* by Rod Clements (HarperCollins, 1997).

GUIDED STUDENT PRACTICE: Use pair share for students to identify the crime (the teeth were stolen), the search for information (all citizens must smile), and the solution (buy new ones, but the real solution is that the dog took them). Have students share their responses.

CLOSURE: Have a student reiterate the crime and solution. Review that the crime is the beginning, the search is the middle, and the solution is the end.

Note: The teacher reinforces the objective by reading at least one picture book mystery a day and having the students identify the crime, the search, and the solution.

MYSTERY LESSON 2: IDENTIFYING THE CLUES AND THE SUSPECTS

REVIEW: The parts of a mystery are the crime (beginning), the search for clues (the middle), and the solution (the end).

OBJECTIVES: Students will identify the clues and suspects in a mystery read aloud.

DIRECT WHOLE GROUP INSTRUCTION: Define clues (bits of information that may help solve the crime) and suspects (the people who may have committed the crime). Read *The Bear Detectives* by Stan and Jan Berenstain (Random, 1975).

GUIDED STUDENT PRACTICE: Using pair share, ask the students to identify the clues in the mystery. After discussing the clues (tracks, pumpkin leaf, prize ribbon, pumpkin seeds, pumpkin smell), ask the students to identify the suspects (cow, pigs, scarecrow), and when they were introduced.

CLOSURE: Have students reiterate the clues.

Note: The teacher reinforces the objective by reading at least one picture book mystery a day and having the students identify the clues and the suspects.

MYSTERY LESSON 3: QUALITIES OF THE INVESTIGATOR

REVIEW: The parts of a mystery are the crime (beginning), the search for clues (the middle), and the solution (the end). Review the meaning of the words "clue" and "suspect."

OBJECTIVES: Students will identify the qualities of the investigator.

DIRECT WHOLE GROUP INSTRUCTION: Explain how to talk about the qualities of the investigator by what he looks like, says, does, what others say about him, and what the author says. Read *Nate the Great* by Marjorie Weinman Sharmat (Coward McCann, 1972).

GUIDED STUDENT PRACTICE: Using pair share, ask the students to identify the qualities of the investigator (Nate) by what he said, did, looked like, what others said about him and what the author said about him. Expected responses are the following: wears a coat and hat, young boy, calls himself "Nate the Great," works alone, likes pancakes, smart (figured out mystery), and Annie asks him for help because she thinks he can solve the mystery.

CLOSURE: Have students reiterate the qualities of the investigator.

Note: The teacher reinforces the objective by reading at least one picture book mystery a day and having the students identify the qualities of the investigator.

LESSON 4: PLOTTING A MYSTERY

REVIEW: The crime is the beginning and the solution is the end of a mystery.

OBJECTIVE: Students will brainstorm crimes and solutions for their own mystery stories.

DIRECT WHOLE GROUP INSTRUCTION: Use pair share to brainstorm ideas for crimes with the teacher. Using a white board or overhead projector, model the process of choosing an idea for a crime and its solution.

GUIDED STUDENT PRACTICE: Use pair share to brainstorm more ideas for crimes. Have the students work in pairs to choose a crime and come up with the solution.

CLOSURE: Some of the students share their crimes and solutions.

MYSTERY LESSON 5: PLANTING THE CLUES AND THE SUSPECTS

REVIEW: Clues are the bits of information that help the investigator solve the crime. Suspects are the people who may have committed the crime.

OBJECTIVE: Students will brainstorm clues and suspects for their own mystery stories.

DIRECT WHOLE GROUP INSTRUCTION: Model pair share with the classroom teacher to brainstorm ideas for clues and suspects using the crime and solution of the day before. Using a white board, smart board, or overhead projector, model the process of choosing clues and suspects and how to plant them in the search for information, the middle of the story.

GUIDED STUDENT PRACTICE: Have the students work with their partners to brainstorm ideas for clues and suspects, then choose clues and suspects, and where to put them in the story.

CLOSURE: Some of the students share their clues and suspects.

Note: The classroom teacher will have the students map their beginning (crime), middle (the search for clues), and end (solution), as well as ensure that the suspects are introduced in the map in the first third of the story.

LESSON PLAN

MYSTERY LESSON 6: CREATING AN INVESTIGATOR

REVIEW: The investigator, the main character, should be a full character with particular looks, speech, and actions.

OBJECTIVE: Students will write a character sketch of the investigator for their mystery story.

DIRECT WHOLE GROUP INSTRUCTION: With the classroom teacher, model how to brainstorm qualities and a name for the investigator modeled in previous lessons. Using a white board, smart board, or overhead projector, model the process of choosing character traits for an investigator. Make sure to include specific idiosyncracies.

GUIDED STUDENT PRACTICE: Have the students work with their partners to brainstorm ideas for qualities, and the name of an investigator for their mystery.

CLOSURE: Some of the students share the qualities and names of their investigators.

Note: The classroom teacher will finish teaching the writing of the character in the classroom as well as teach the rest of the writing process to finish the mystery story if a finished product is desired.

MYSTERY BEGINNER AND PICTURE BOOKS

Adler, David A., *Young Cam Jansen and the Dinosaur Game.* Viking, 1996.
Platt, Kin, *Big Max in the Mystery of the Missing Moose.* Harper & Row , 1977.
Sharmat, Marjorie Weinman, *Nate the Great and the Lost List.* Coward, McCann, 1975.
Yolen, Jane, *Picnic with Piggins.* Harcourt Brace, 1988.

MYSTERY NOVELS

Byars, Betsy, *The Dark Stairs.* Viking, 1994, 130pp.
Bunting, Eve, *Nasty, Stinky Sneakers.* HarperCollins, 1994, 105pp.
Haddix, Margaret Peterson, *Running Out of Time.* Simon & Schuster, 1995, 184pp.
Wallace, Barbara, *Cousins in the Castle.* Atheneum, 1996, 152pp.
Wright, Betty Ren, *Too Many Secrets.* Scholastic, 1997, 116pp.

▷ FANTASY

According to Dean Koontz, in *Writing Popular Fiction* (Writer's Digest, 1974), fantasy is literature that deals with magic and the supernatural. It does not have a reasonable or scientific basis like science fiction. The things and people in a fantasy cannot really happen. There may be charms, spells, and curses. There may be nonhuman characters, such as ghosts, witches, sorcerers, and elves. Usually it takes place in a world unlike our own. There is no need to explain how this world came to be. Once the place or situation has been created, however, the characters and events must be logical. The story may involve a quest, which requires the hero to go on a journey. Many times the conflict is good versus evil. A good reference for teaching fantasy is *Bringing Fantasy Alive for Children and Young Adults* by Tim Wadham and Rachel Wadham (Linworth, 1999).

One type of fantasy is animal fantasy, where animals talk and sometimes behave like human beings. Many of the first picture books for children are animal fantasies, such as *The Runaway Bunny* by Margaret Wise Brown (Harper & Row, 1972,1942).

Perhaps the most popular type of fantasy is the ghost story. Even the youngest children enjoy the surprise in *The Dark, Dark Room and Other Scary Tales* by Alvin Schwartz (HarperCollins, 1984).

FANTASY LESSON 1: IDENTIFYING THE FANTASTIC

REVIEW: When you watch cartoons, do the things and people you see happen in real life?

OBJECTIVE: Students will identify the elements of fantasy in a story read to them.

DIRECT WHOLE GROUP INSTRUCTION: Explain the objective and give an example of the different elements of fantasy: places, nonhuman characters, magic, and the hero's quest. Read *Harvey Potter's Balloon Farm* by Jerdine Nolen Harold (Lothrop, Lee & Shepard, 1993), and *Chocolatina* by Erik Kraft (Bridge Water, 1998).

GUIDED STUDENT PRACTICE: Use pair share for students to identify the elements of fantasy in the stories read. Have students share their responses. (*Harvey Potter's Balloon Farm* is a fantastic place, *Chocolatina* is magic).

CLOSURE: Have a student reiterate some of the fantastic elements of the book.

Note: The teacher reinforces the objective by reading at least one picture book fantasy a day and having the students identify the elements of fantasy in the setting and characters. These picture books can come from the preceding bibliography, a bibliography compiled by the library media specialist, or the library's catalog.

FANTASY LESSON 2: COMPARING NONFICTION ANIMAL BOOKS WITH ANIMAL FANTASY BOOKS

REVIEW: What things can a cartoon animal do in a cartoon that real animals cannot do in real life?

OBJECTIVE: Students will identify how an animal's real characteristics are used in an animal fantasy.

DIRECT WHOLE GROUP INSTRUCTION: Explain the objective. Read *Ten Things I Know About Penguins* by Wendy Wax and Della Rowland (Contemporary, 1989) and *Tacky in Trouble* by Helen Lester (Houghton Mifflin, 1998).

GUIDED STUDENT PRACTICE: Use pair share for students to identify the real characteristics of penguins and the things that Tacky could do that real penguins can and cannot do as reflected in *Tacky in Trouble*. Have students share their responses. Expected responses:

Real: Belly slide, live on ice, hop, march

Fantastic: Talk, backslap, surf, wear a flowered shirt

CLOSURE: Have a student reiterate some of the real penguin characteristics or habits that were shown in *Tacky in Trouble*.

Note: Each day to reinforce the objective, the teacher reads an animal fantasy picture book and a book about the real animal and has students identify the real characteristics and habits as shown in the fantasy.

Some suggested pairings are as follows:

Bats by Lynn M. Stone (Rourke, 1993) or *Squeaking Bats* by Ruth Berman (Lerner, 1998) and *Stellaluna* by Janell Cannon (Harcourt Brace, 1993)

Chickens by Peter Brady (Capstone, 1996) and *Hilda Hen's Scary Night* by Mary Wormell (Harcourt Brace, 1996)

Cows by Peter Brady (Capstone, 1996) and *When Bluebell Sang* by Lisa Campbell Ernst (Bradbury, 1989) or *When Minnie and Moo Go Dancing* by Denys Cazet (DK, 1998)

Duckling Days by Karen Wallace (DK, 1999) and *Happy Birthday, Dear Duck* by Eve Bunting (Clarion, 1988)

Fishing Bears by Ruth Berman (Lerner, 1998) and *Good Job, Little Bear!* by Martin Waddell (Candlewick, 1999)

Pigs by Peter Brady (Capstone, 1996) and *Oink* by Arthur Geisert (Houghton Mifflin, 1991)

Sheep by Peter Brady (Capstone, 1996) and *Sheep in a Jeep* by Nancy Shaw (Houghton Mifflin, 1986)

LESSON PLAN

FANTASY LESSON 3: CREATING A FANTASTIC PLACE OR PERSON

REVIEW: Ask students the settings in the fantasy books read in the past week by the library media specialist and the teacher.

OBJECTIVE: Students will brainstorm settings for their own fantasy stories.

DIRECT WHOLE GROUP INSTRUCTION: Model pair share with the teacher to brainstorm ideas for fantastic settings. Using a white board, smart board, or overhead projector, model the process of choosing an idea for a fantastic setting and adding important details. Be graphic and draw a map or diagram of the place.

GUIDED STUDENT PRACTICE: Use pair share to brainstorm more ideas for fantastic settings. Have the students work in pairs to choose a setting and add important details.

CLOSURE: Some of the students share their settings.

Note: The teacher has the students refine their fantastic settings in the classroom using paragraphs and pictures. The teacher reinforces the objective by reading at least one picture book fantasy a day from the preceding bibliography, one compiled by the library media specialist, or one chosen from the library's catalog. The students identify the elements of fantasy in the setting and characters in these books.

FANTASY LESSON 4: CREATING A FANTASTIC CHARACTER

REVIEW: Ask the students what types of fantastic characters (supernatural, animals, people with superpowers) were in the fantasy books read in the past week by the library media specialist and the teacher.

OBJECTIVE: Students will brainstorm fantastic characters

DIRECT WHOLE GROUP INSTRUCTION: Model pair share with the teacher to brainstorm ideas for fantastic characters. Using a white board or overhead projector, model the process of choosing an idea for a fantastic character and adding important details about appearance, actions, speech, and special powers to write a character sketch.

GUIDED STUDENT PRACTICE: Use pair share to brainstorm more ideas for fantastic characters. Have the students work in pairs to choose a character and add important details to write a character sketch.

CLOSURE: Some of the students share their characters.

Note: The classroom teacher will finish teaching the writing of the character sketch and give the students the resources to draw an accompanying picture. The teacher may want to have the students make up a story using either their fantastic place or fantastic character, or both.

FANTASY PICTURE BOOKS

Carle, Eric, *The Grouchy Ladybug.* HarperCollins, 1996.

Kraft, Erik, *Chocolatina.* BridgeWater, 1998.

Loredo, Elizabeth, *Boogie Bones.* Putnam, 1997.

Marshall, James, *George and Martha.* Houghton Mifflin, 1972.

Meddaugh, Susan, *Martha Speaks.* Houghton Mifflin, 1992.

Nicole-Lisa, W., *Shake Dem Halloween Bones.* Houghton Mifflin, 1997.

Pilkey, Dav, *Hallo-weiner.* Blue Sky Press, 1995.

Pinkwater, Daniel, *Young Larry.* Marshall Cavendish, 1997.

Schwartz, Alvin, *In a Dark, Dark Room and Other Scary Tales.* HarperCollins, 1984.

Sendak, Maurice, *Where the Wild Things Are.* Harper, 1963.

Seuss, Dr., *And to Think That I Saw It on Mulberry Street.* Vanguard, 1937.

Turkle, Brinton, *Do Not Open.* Dutton, 1981.

Wells, Rosemary, *Bunny Cakes.* Dial, 1997.

FANTASY NOVELS

Alexander, Lloyd, *Westmark.* Dutton, 1981, 184pp.

Avi, *Poppy.* Orchard, 1995, 146pp.

Howe, Deborah, *Bunnicula.* Atheneum, 1979, 98pp.

King-Smith, Dick, *The School Mouse.* Hyperion, 1995, 123pp.

Levine, Gail Carson, *Ella Enchanted.* HarperCollins, 1997, 232pp.

Naylor, Phyllis, *Sang Spell.* Athenuem, 1998, 176pp.

Rowling, J.K., *Harry Potter and the Chamber of Secrets,* Arthur A. Levine, 1999, 341pp.

Rowling, J.K., *Harry Potter and the Goblet of Fire.* Arthur A. Levine, 2000, 734pp.

Rowling, J.K., *Harry Potter and the Prisoner of Azkaban.* Arthur A. Levine, 1999, 435pp.

Rowling, J.K., *Harry Potter and the Sorcerer's Stone.* Arthur A. Levine, 1998, 309pp.

⮞ SCIENCE FICTION

Robert Heinlein writes in a chapter of *Science Fiction and Fantasy*, edited by Gardner Dozois et al. (St. Martin's Press, 1991), that science fiction is about either people or gadgets. If it's about people, then the living conditions are different from current day, and the condition must be an essential part of the story. The problem is how the humans react and live under these new conditions. However, in making these new conditions, no proven facts can be ignored.

The Young Reader's Companion by Gorton Carruth (Bowker, 1993) asserts that science fiction is based on scientific fact, and how humans will be affected by scientific advances.

LESSON PLAN

SCIENCE FICTION LESSON 1: IDENTIFYING THE FICTION PART OF SCIENCE FICTION

REVIEW: When you watch Science Fiction on television and in movies, do the things and people you see happen in real life?

OBJECTIVE: Students will identify the elements of science fiction in stories read to them.

DIRECT WHOLE GROUP INSTRUCTION: Explain the objective and give an example of the different elements of science fiction: places, aliens, and gadgets. Read *Smile If You're Human* by Neal Layton (Dial, 1999) and *The Banana Split from Outer Space* by Catherine Siracusa (Hyperion, 1995).

GUIDED STUDENT PRACTICE: Use pair share for students to identify the elements of science fiction in the stories read. Have students share their responses such as space ships, aliens, and root beer as fuel.

CLOSURE: Have a student reiterate some of the science fiction elements of the book.

LESSON PLAN

SCIENCE FICTION LESSON 2: CREATING AN ALIEN CHARACTER

REVIEW: Ask the students what types of science fiction elements (inventions, aliens, space travel) were in the science fiction books read in the past week by the library media specialist and the teacher.

OBJECTIVE: Students will describe an alien they have imagined.

DIRECT WHOLE GROUP INSTRUCTION: Model pair share with the teacher to brainstorm ideas for alien characters. Use a white board, overhead projector, data projector or smart board to model the process of choosing an idea for an alien and adding important details about appearance, actions, speech, and special powers to write a character sketch.

GUIDED STUDENT PRACTICE: Use pair share to brainstorm more ideas for alien characters. Have the students work in pairs to choose a character and add important details to write a character sketch.

CLOSURE: Some of the students share their characters.

Note: The classroom teacher will finish teaching the character sketch writing lesson and give students the resources to draw an accompanying picture. The teacher may want to have the students make up a story using the alien as a main character.

SCIENCE FICTION LESSON 3: CREATING A GADGET

REVIEW: Ask the students about the gadgets in the science fiction books read in the past week by the library media specialist and the teacher.

OBJECTIVE: Students will create a gadget that would make life on earth different.

DIRECT WHOLE GROUP INSTRUCTION: Model pair share with the teacher to brainstorm ideas for gadgets that would change life on earth. Use a white board, overhead projector, data projector or smart board to model the process of choosing an idea for a gadget and adding important details about what it looks like, how it works, and how it would change life on earth.

GUIDED STUDENT PRACTICE: Use pair share to brainstorm more ideas for gadgets. Have the students work in pairs to choose a gadget and add important details. The students should sketch out their gadgets and write a few sentences about what it can do.

CLOSURE: Some of the students share their ideas for gadgets.

Note: The classroom teacher will finish teaching the writing of the gadget description. The teacher may want to have the students make up a story using the gadget to create a conflict for a plot.

SCIENCE FICTION EASY READERS AND PICTURE BOOKS

Layton, Neal, *Smile If You're Human.* Dial, 1999.

McPhail, David, *Tinker and Tom and the Star Baby.* Little, Brown, 1998.

Siracusa, Catherine, *The Banana Split from Outer Space.* Hyperion, 1995.

Weisner, David, *June 29, 1999.* Clarion, 1992.

Willis, Jeanne, *The Long Blue Blazer.* Dutton, 1987.

Yaccarino, Dan, *Zoom! Zoom! Zoom! I'm Off to the Moon!* Scholastic, 1997.

Yolen, Jane, *Commander Toad and the Planet of the Grapes.* Coward McCann, 1982.

SCIENCE FICTION NOVELS

Coville, Bruce, *Aliens Ate My Homework.* Pocket, 1993, 179pp.

L'Engle, Madeleine, *A Wrinkle in Time.* Farrar, 1962, 203pp.

Lowry, Lois, *The Giver.* Houghton Mifflin, 1993, 180pp.

Pinkwater, Daniel Manus*, Fat Men from Space.* Putnam, 1990, 1977, 57pp.

Pope, Mary Osborne, *Vacation Under the Volcano.* Random, 1998, 80pp.

▷ HISTORICAL FICTION

Historical fiction has all the elements of a mainstream novel except that it is set in the past. The focus is on the character or the period. Most students do not have the historical background to judge whether the period is portrayed accurately. Rather, they can observe everyday life in the historical period and compare it with their lives today. This genre is the easiest to integrate into the social studies curriculum. Students can be exposed to concepts and ways of life in an exciting and personal way. The main character is someone with whom the student can identify.

HISTORICAL FICTION LESSON 1: COMPARING TODAY WITH ANOTHER TIME IN HISTORY

REVIEW: How have things changed in the last 50 years? Give examples from the childhood of the library media specialist, such as the advent of color TV, microwave ovens, computers, videos, people in space, and no sports for girls.

OBJECTIVE: Students will compare aspects of their lives to those of the historical period in the stories read to them.

DIRECT WHOLE GROUP INSTRUCTION: Explain the objective and give an example of the different elements, such as appliances, roles of women, how people treated each other, or transportation when the library media specialist was younger. Read *Sweet Clara and the Freedom Quilt* by Deborah Hopkinson (Knopf, 1993) and *The Quilt Story* by Tony Johnston (Putnam, 1985).

GUIDED STUDENT PRACTICE: Using pair share, have students compare life in each story with life today.

CLOSURE: Have a student reiterate the historical elements of the stories read.

HISTORICAL FICTION LESSON 2: TIME TRAVELER

REVIEW: Historical fiction is a story told during another time in history.

OBJECTIVE: Students will evaluate the advantages and disadvantages of living during the gold rush.

DIRECT WHOLE GROUP INSTRUCTION: Read *The Legend of Freedom Hill* by Linda Jacobs Altman (Lee & Low, 2000).

GUIDED STUDENT PRACTICE: Using pair share, have students compare what would be good and bad about living in the American West during the gold rush. Advantages might include the following: Children have more freedom to go out, anyone could strike it rich, friendships were close, families were close. Disadvantages might be the following: Slavery still existed, people were discriminated against on the basis of race and religion.

CLOSURE: Have students reiterate the advantages and disadvantages of living during the gold rush.

HISTORICAL FICTION PICTURE BOOKS (THE ONES FOR OLDER STUDENTS ARE ASTERISKED)

Altman, Linda Jacobs, *The Legend of Freedom Hill.* Lee & Low, 2000.

*Bunting, Eve, *The Blue and the Gray.* Scholastic, 1996.

Corey, Shana, *You Forgot Your Skirt, Amelia Bloomer!: A Very Improper Story.* Scholastic, 2000.

Hearne, Betsy, *Seven Brave Women.* Greenwillow, 1997

Hopkinson, Deborah, *Sweet Clara and the Freedom Quilt.* Knopf, 1993.

Kirkpatrick, Katherine, *Redcoats and Petticoats.* Holiday House, 1999.

Lorbiecki, Mary Beth. *Sister Anne's Hands.* Dial, 1998.

McCully, Emily Arnold, *Popcorn at the Palace.* Harcourt Brace, 1997.

*Nerlove, Miriam, *Flowers on the Wall.* Margaret K. Elderberry, 1996.

*Pollacco, Patricia, *Pink and Say.* Philomel, 1994.

Shea, Pegi Deitz, *The Whispering Cloth.* Boyds Mills, 1995.

Stanley, Diane, *Saving Sweetness.* Putnam, 1996.

Woodruff, Elvira, *The Memory Coat.* Scholastic, 1999.

*Yolen, Jane, *Encounter.* Harcourt Brace, 1992.

HISTORICAL FICTION NOVELS

Burks, Brian, *Walks Alone.* Harcourt Brace, 1998, 115pp.

Curtis, Christopher, *Bud, Not Buddy.* Delacorte, 1999, 245pp.

Cushman, Karen, *Catherine, Called Birdy.* Clarion, 1994, 169pp.

Erdich, Louise, *The Birchbark House,* Hyperion, 1999, 244pp.

Hesse, Karen, *Letters from Rifka.* Holt, 1992, 148pp.

MacLachan, Patricia, *Sarah Plain and Tall.* Harper & Row, 1985, 58pp.

McKissack, Patricia C., *Run Away Home.* Scholastic, 1997, 160pp.

O'Dell, Scott, *Sing Down the Moon.* Dell, 1989, 1971, 124pp.

Patrick, Denise Lewis, *The Adventures of Midnight Son.* Holt, 1997, 152pp.

Paulsen, Gary, *Mr. Tucket.* Delacorte, 1994, 166pp.

Peck, Richard, *A Long Way from Chicago.* Dial, 1998, 148pp.

Rosen, Michael J., *A School for Pompey Walker.* Harcourt Brace, 1995, 48pp.

Ryan, Pam Munoz, *Riding Freedom.* Scholastic, 1998, 138pp.

Taylor, Mildred, *Song of the Trees.* Dial, 1975, 48pp.

Woodruff, Elvira, *Dear Austin: Letters from the Underground Railroad.* Knopf, 1998, 137 pp.

◣ CONTEMPORARY REALISM

This genre reflects things that could happen now. Students can compare their lives with those in the books and gain insights into their own problems. These books usually speak to the themes of belonging, loving and being loved, the need for competence, family relationships, peer relationships, and the importance of friendship. They also deal with the problems of city life, child abuse, death, and divorce. The characters are more likely to be of diverse backgrounds. The lesson plans for this genre can be the same as those on main idea and theme in Chapter Six.

LESSON PLAN FOR CONTEMPORARY REALISM

REVIEW: Contemporary realism is a story that happens in the current time.

OBJECTIVE: Students will write a fictional account, based on an incident in their lives.

DIRECT WHOLE GROUP INSTRUCTION: Using a white board, overhead or data projector, or smart board, model how to brainstorm ideas for an incident on which to base a contemporary realism story. Write at least three ideas from the library media specialist's life. Choose one of the ideas and write notes on details: setting, how to make the characters fictional, emotions, events of beginning, middle and end. Then use the notes to write a contemporary realism story of several paragraphs.

GUIDED PRACTICE: Have the students first brainstorm three ideas for incidents on which to base a contemporary realistic story. Have them share these ideas with a partner. Give each pair a worksheet with the following questions:

- When did this happen?
- Where did it happen? What are some details about this place?
- Who is involved besides you? How can you change the characters to make them fictional?
- What happens first? What happens next? What happens at the end?
- What emotions do the characters feel?
- One partner asks the detail questions while the other partner records his or her own answers.

CLOSURE: Ask for a show of hands as to when the incident they wrote about happened: This week? Last week? Last month? Last year? Two years ago? Five years ago? Reiterate that all of these settings are considered "contemporary."

Note: The teacher can continue working with the students on their stories in the classroom.

CONTEMPORARY REALISM PICTURE BOOKS

Barber, Barbara E., *Allie's Basketball Dream.* Lee & Lothrop, 1996.

Bunting, Eve, *Your Move.* Harcourt Brace, 1998.

Cowley, Joy, *Big Moon Tortillas.* Boyds Mills, 1998.

Grimes, Nikki, *My Man Blue.* Dial, 1999.

Haller, Danita. *Not Just Any Ring.* Knopf, 1982.

Hoffman, Mary*, Amazing Grace.* Dial, 1991.

Polacco, Patricia, *My Rotten Redheaded Brother.* Simon & Schuster, 1994.

Raczek, Linda Theresa, *The Night the Grandfathers Danced.* Northland, 1995.

Raczek, Linda Theresa, *Rainy's Pow Wow.* Rising Moon, 1999.

Scott, Ann Herbert, *Brave as a Mountain Lion.* Clarion, 1996.

Sharmat, Marjorie Weinman, *Gila Monsters Meet You at the Airport.* Macmillan, 1980.

Soto, Gary, *Too Many Tamales.* Putnam, 1996.

CONTEMPORARY REALISM NOVELS

Belton, Sandra, *Ernestine & Amanda: Summer Camp Ready or Not!* Simon & Schuster, 1996, 160pp

Bolden, Tonya, *Just Family.* Dutton, 1996, 149pp.

Carbine, Elisa Lynn, *Starting School with an Enemy.* Knopf, 1998, 103pp.

Danzinger, Paula, *Amber Brown Is Not a Crayon.* Putnam, 1994, 80pp.

Jimenez, Francis O., *The Circuit.* University of New Mexico, 1997, 134pp.

Konigsburg, E. L., *The View from Saturday.* Atheneum, 1996, 163pp.

Hesse, Karen, *Just Juice.* Scholastic, 1998, 138pp.

Holt, Kimberly Willis, *My Louisiana Sky.* Holt, 1998, 200pp.

Mead, Alice, *Junebug.* Farrar, 1995, 101pp.

Parks, Barbara, *Mick Harte Was Here.* Knopf, 1995, 89pp.

Sachar, Louis, *Holes.* Farrar, 1998, 233pp.

Taylor, Bonnie Highsmith, *Tall Shadow.* Perfection, 1998, 92pp.

Voigt, Cynthia, *Bad Girls.* Scholastic, 1996, 277pp.

CHAPTER 10

Poetry

Poetry is a form of literature feared by many teachers and school library media specialists. The purpose of this chapter is to integrate poetry into storytime and use it to teach reading. Poetry is most easily inserted in storytimes that are planned by subject. Remember to include poems that are famous to you but may be unknown to the students. Many of the poetry books have subject indices. One of the best ways to find poetry that fits is to read it. Peruse the books in the 811–821 sections of the library.

▷ COLLABORATION

When collaborating with the kindergarten teachers on what topics to include in story-time, remember to search for a few good poems. Many poems are available in picture book format. If the topic is farms, try *Over on the Farm* by Christopher Gunson (Scholastic, 1997) as well as poems about the farm animals, such as *On the Farm* edited by Lee Bennett Hopkins (Little, Brown, 1991). If the topic is oceanography, try *Splish Splash* by Joan Bransfield Graham (Ticknor & Fields, 1994), *In the Swim* by Douglas Florian (Harcourt, 1997), or "If I Were a Fish" by Karla Kuskin in her poetry book *The Sky Is Always in the Sky* (HarperCollins, 1998). If the topic is dinosaurs, try *Tyrannosaurus Was a Beast* by Jack Prelutsky (Greenwillow, 1988), *Dinosaurs Forever* by William Wise (Dail, 2000), or *Dinosaurs,* edited by Lee Bennett Hopkins (Harcourt, Brace, Javonovich, 1987).

➤ LITERARY ELEMENTS

Literary elements can be found in most narrative poetry. *The Adventures of Isabel* by Ogden Nash (Little, Brown, 1991) and "Grandmother" in *Navajo Visions and Voices Across the Mesa* by Shonto Begay (Scholastic, 1995) are excellent resources for the study of character. If Arnold Lobel's *Frog and Toad* series are used to study character, include "Toad and Frog Reel" from *The Reptile Ball* by Jacqueline K. Ogburn (Dial, 1997). Setting is well described in "Snow City" by Lee Bennett Hopkins in his book *Good Rhymes, Good Times* (HarperCollins, 1995). Plot conflict is evident in "I, Too, Sing America" by Langston Hughes, found in a collection of the same name edited by Catherine Clinton (Houghton Mifflin, 1998). Other poems with conflicts are "Old Snake" by Pat Mora in her book *This Big Sky* (Scholastic, 1998) and "Gum Drop" by Douglas Florian in his book *Laugh-eteria* (Harcourt Brace, 1999). One of the best ways to teach theme is to use poems such as "Willie Ate a Worm Today" by Jack Prelutsky in his book *Rolling Harvey Down the Hill* (Greenwillow, 1980).

➤ GENRE

Poetry can be included when teaching genre. When introducing mystery to intermediate or junior high students, consider prefacing the storytime with "The Raven" by Edgar Allen Poe (*Tales and Poems of Edgar Allan Poe,* Macmillan, 1963). For fantasy, consider some Edward Lear, Jack Prelutsky, or Lewis Carroll's "Jabberwocky" from *Through the Looking Glass.* The latter is available in picture book form, *Jabberwocky* (H.N. Abrams, 1989,1897). For historical fiction, try using *The Midnight Ride of Paul Revere* by Henry Wadsworth Longfellow (Dutton, 1990) or a poem from *Hand in Hand: An American History Through Poetry* collected by Lee Bennett Hopkins (Simon & Schuster, 1994). For realistic fiction, try using *Casey at the Bat* by Ernest Laurence Thayer (Coward, McCann, 1978) as an example of how everything doesn't always turn out right.

➤ NONFICTION

Consider using poetry to compare with a nonfiction book to see what facts have been woven into the poem. Some poems are included in the lesson in Chapter Eleven entitled "Finding facts in fiction and poetry." Poems are also included in the lesson comparing nonfiction books.

Additional Poetry Titles that Are Useful for Storytime:

Arbuthnot, May Hill and Shelton, L. Root Jr., *Time for Poetry*. Scott, Foresman, 1968.
Bauer, Caroline Feller, *The Poetry Break*. H.W. Wilson, 1994.
Prelutsky, Jack, *Random House Book of Poetry for Children*. Random, 1983.

CHAPTER 11

Nonfiction

▷ OBJECTIVES

The notion of using nonfiction in storytime is not new, but it is sometimes forgotten amid all the fiction. Two major objectives can be taught with nonfiction. The first is that students will distinguish between fiction and nonfiction. The second comes from chapter two of *IP 2*, the information literacy standards, which require that students evaluate information.

These objectives can be woven into storytimes. One of the best ways is to collaborate with the classroom teachers about their units of study, so nonfiction storytimes can be coordinated with the content being taught in the classroom. It is also possible to choose topics by which books and materials the teachers request from the library media center. The first lesson teaches students to distinguish between fiction and nonfiction. The second lesson deals with evaluating nonfiction. Most students would find it difficult, if not impossible, to evaluate nonfiction for accuracy, writing style, and objectivity. Even the youngest students are quite capable, however, of comparing the facts and styles in several nonfiction books on the same topic.

NONFICTION LESSON 1: DISTINGUISHING NONFICTION FROM FICTION

REVIEW: Ask the students to give examples of a fact and a story. Supply examples that begin the same way. For instance, going to the store for the groceries and how much each item costs, and going to the store with a pet dinosaur.

OBJECTIVE: Students will be able to tell which book is fiction and which is nonfiction.

DIRECT WHOLE GROUP INSTRUCTION: Explain the objective and give definitions of the words "fiction" and "nonfiction." Read a fiction book and a nonfiction book on a topic that the class is currently studying. (Sometimes the nonfiction book is too long for sharing. If so, choose the most interesting part of the book to read aloud). Listed below are some suggestions for topics.

STUDENT PRACTICE: Use pair share for students to identify which book emphasizes facts and which book emphasizes story, with specifics to back up their answers. Have students share their responses.

CLOSURE: Have students chorally reiterate the definitions of "fiction" and "nonfiction."

PAIRINGS OF FICTION/NONFICTION BOOKS BY TOPIC:

Unbeatable Bread by Lyn Littlefield Hoopes (Dial, 1996) and *Bakers* by Tami Deedrick (Capstone, 1998)

Softchild: How Rattlesnake Got Its Fangs by Joe Hayes (Harbinger House, 1993) and *All About Rattlesnakes* by Jim Arnosky (Scholastic, 1997)

Ginger by Charlotte Voake (Candlewick, 1997) and *Cats* by Gail Gibbons (Holiday House, 1996)

The Great White Man-Eating Shark by Margaret Mahy (Dial, 1990) and *Hungry, Hungry Sharks* by Joanna Cole (Random, 1986) and "The Sharks" by Douglas Florian in his book *In the Swim* (Harcourt Brace, 1997)

Big Moon Tortilla by Joy Cowley (Boyds Mills, 1998) and *Tortilla Factory* by Gary Paulsen (Harcourt Brace, 1995)

NONFICTION LESSON 2: FINDING FACTS IN FICTION AND POETRY (SIMILAR TO FANTASY LESSON 2)

REVIEW: Ask the students what the differences are between "fiction" and "nonfiction."

OBJECTIVE: Students will discern which parts of a fiction book were based on facts.

DIRECT WHOLE GROUP INSTRUCTION: Explain that fiction writers often do research so that their characters, although imaginary, behave in some ways like a real person or a real animal. Ask the students to look for such facts while you are reading both a fiction and a nonfiction book on a topic that the class is currently studying. Read the nonfiction book first. (Sometimes the nonfiction book is too long for sharing. If so, choose the parts of the nonfiction book that include facts that the author of the fiction book has woven into the story). Below are listed some suggestions for topics.

STUDENT PRACTICE: Use pair share for students to identify which facts from the nonfiction book were included in the fiction story. Have students share their responses.

CLOSURE: Have students chorally respond to the definitions of "fiction" and "nonfiction."

PAIRINGS AND GROUPINGS OF NONFICTION/FICTION BOOKS BY TOPICS:

Dinosaurs: *Tyrannosaurus Rex* by Daniel Petersen (Childrens, 1989) and *Tyrone the Terrible* by Hans Wilhelm (Scholastic, 1988)

Space exploration: *Man on the Moon* by Anastasia Suen (Viking, 1997) and *Zoom! Zoom! Zoom! I'm Off to the Moon* by Dan Yaccarino (Scholastic, 1997)

Slavery: *To Be a Slave* by Julius Lester (Dial, 1998) and *Journey to Freedom* by Courtni Wright (Holiday House, 1994)

Zoo animals: *My Visit to the Zoo* by Aliki (HarperCollins, 1997) and *If Anything Ever Goes Wrong at the Zoo* by Mary Jean Hendrick (Harcourt Brace, 1993)

Elephants: *Elmer* by David McKee (Lopthrop, 1989), *Elephants* by Claire Robinson (Heinemann Library, 1997), "The Elephant" in *Cats and Bats and Things with Wings* by Conrad Aiken (Atheneum, 1966), and "The Handiest Nose" by Aileen Fisher in *Side by Side: Poems to Read Together,* collected by Lee Bennett Hopkins (Simon & Schuster, 1988)

Hospitals: *Going to the Hospital* by Fred Rogers (Putnam, 1988) and *Franklin Goes to the Hospital* by Paulette Bourgeois (Kids Can, 2000)

Farms: *Farming* by Gail Gibbons (Holiday House, 1988) and *The Day Jimmy's Boa Ate the Wash* by Trina Hakes Noble (Dial, 1984,1980)

Immigration: *Coming to America* by Betsy Maestro (Scholastic, 1996) and *When Jessie Came Across the Sea* by Amy Hest (Candlewick, 1997)

NONFICTION LESSON 3: COMPARING THE INFORMATION IN NONFICTION BOOKS

REVIEW: Nonfiction is a book of facts.

OBJECTIVE: Students will be able to compare the facts in two nonfiction books for scope and for discrepancies.

DIRECT WHOLE GROUP INSTRUCTION: Explain the objective and that "scope" means which part of a subject the author has chosen to write about. Read two nonfiction books on a subject that the class is currently studying. (Sometimes the nonfiction books are too long for sharing. If so, choose parts of the books that cover some of the same facts.) Below are listed some suggestions for books on particular subjects.

STUDENT PRACTICE: Use pair share for students to identify if the facts of the two books are the same. Have students share their responses. If some facts are not the same, consult a third source, such as the encyclopedia, to compare the information of a specific fact. Then ask students if the "scope" was the same in both books. Did the authors write about the same or different aspects of the topic?

CLOSURE: Have students chorally reiterate the definitions of "nonfiction."

PAIRINGS OF NONFICTION BOOKS BY SUBJECTS:

Cowboys: *Cowboy Country* by Ann Herbert Scott (Clarion, 1993) and *A Day in the Life of a Cowboy* by Alvin G. Davis (Troll, 1991)

Dinosaurs' demise: *Tyrannosaurus Rex* by Elaine Landau (Children's Press, 1999) and *What Happened to the Dinosaurs?* By Franklyn M. Branley (Crowell, 1989)

Hurricanes: *Storms* by Ray Broekel (Childrens Press, 1982), *Hurricanes* by Arlene Erlbach (Childrens Press, 1993) and *Hurricanes* by D.M. Sousa (Carolrhoda, 1996)

Johnny Appleseed: *Johnny Appleseed* by Steven Kellogg (Morrow, 1988) and *The Story of Johnny Appleseed* by Aliki (Prentice Hall, 1963)

Sharks: *Sharks* by Gail Gibbons (Holiday House, 1992) and *Sharks, Sharks, Sharks* by Tina Anton (Raintree, 1989)

Conclusion

The future of library media specialists is in jeopardy. Professional positions have been eliminated during budget crunches and pushes for smaller class sizes. By becoming part of the instructional program, school library media specialists can become indispensable educational leaders.

School library media specialists become educational leaders when they use storytime to teach reading and writing if

- the objectives are performance based;
- the objectives are based on local, state, and national standards that drive the school's curriculum;
- active participation strategies are used;
- there is collaboration with classroom teachers with respect to methods, content, and objectives; and
- the administration and staff know it is happening.

Each person can make a difference, one storytime at a time.

Bibliography of Professional Works Cited

American Association of School Librarians, *Information Power: Building Partnerships for Learning.* American Library Association, 1998, 205 pp.

Anderson, Dee, *Amazingly Easy Puppet Plays.* American Library Association, 1997, 235pp.

Anderson, Paul S., *Storytelling with the Flannel Board.* Dennison, 1963, 220 pp.

Association for Library Service to Children, *The Newberry and Caldecott Awards:*

A Guide to the Medal and Honor Books. American Library Association, 2000, 167pp.

Barchers, Suzanne I., *Multicultural Folktales: Readers Theatre for Elementary Students.* Libraries Unlimited, 2000, 188pp.

Bauer, Caroline Feller, *The Poetry Break.* H.W. Wilson, 1994, 347 pp.

Carruth, Gorton, *The Young Reader's Companion.* Bowker, 1993, 681 pp.

Dozois, Gardner, ed., *Writing Science Fiction and Fantasy.* St. Martin's, 1991, 264 pp.

Dundes, Alan, *The Study of Folklore.* Prentice Hall, 1965, 481pp.

Farmer, Lesley S. J., *Workshops for Teachers: Becoming Partners for Information Literacy.* Linworth, 1995, 142pp.

Forster, E. M., *Aspects of the Novel.* Harcourt, 1985, 1927, 176 pp.

Gerke, Pamela, *Multicultural Plays for Children Volume 1: Grades K–3.* Smith and Kraus, 1999, 161pp.

Gerke, Pamela, *Multicultural Plays for Children Volume 2: Grades 4–6.* Smith and Kraus, 1999, 161pp.

Glandon, Shan, *Caldecott Connections to Language Arts.* Libraries Unlimited, 2000, 232pp.

Glandon, Shan, *Caldecott Connections to Science.* Libraries Unlimited, 2000, 228pp.

Glandon, Shan, *Caldecott Connections to Social Studies.* Libraries Unlimited, 2000, 161pp.

Gronlund, Norman E., *How to Write and Use Instructional Objectives.* Merrill, 2000, 126 pp.

Hamilton-Pennell, Christine; Lance, Keith Curry; Rodney, Narcia; Hainer, Eugene; "Dick and Jane Go to the Head of the Class," *School Library Journal,* April 1, 2000, pp. 44–47.

Hunter, Madeline, *Mastery Teaching.* Corwin Press, 1982, 113pp.

Koontz, Dean, *Writing Popular Fiction.* Writers Digest, 1972, 232pp.

Krashen, Stephen, *The Power of Reading.* Libraries Unlimited, 1993, 119pp.

Loertscher, David V., *Taxonomies of the School Library Media Program.* Hi Willow, 2000, 258pp.

Lukens, Rebecca, *A Critical Handbook of Children's Literature.* Harper Collins, 1999, 368pp.

McKenzie, Jamie, *Beyond Technology: Questioning, Research and the Information Literate School.* FNO Press, 2000, 168pp.

Miller, Donna P. and Anderson, J'Lynn Anderson, *Developing an Integrated Library Program.* Linworth, 1996, 197pp.

Roberts, Gillian, *You Can Write a Mystery.* Writers Digest, 1999, 124pp.

Sawyer, Ruth, *The Way of the Storyteller.* Viking, 1962, 360pp.

Shedlock, Marie, *The Art of the Storyteller.* Dover, 1951, 290pp.

Sierra, Judy, *The Flannel Board Storytelling Book.* H.W. Wilson, 1987, 203pp.

Sierra, Judy, *Multicultural Folktales for the Feltboard and Readers' Theater.* Oryx, 1996, 186pp.

Sierra, Judy, and Kiminski, Robert, *Multicultural Folktales: Stories to Tell Young Children.* Oryx, 1991, 126pp.

Trelease, Jim, *The Read Aloud Handbook.* Penguin, 1995, 387 pp.

Volz, Bridget Dealy, Scheer, Cheryl Perkins, and Wellborn, Lynda Blackburn, *Junior Genreflecting: A Guide to Good Reads and Series Fiction for Children.* Libraries Unlimited, 2000, 187pp

Wadham, Tim and Wadham, Rachel L., *Bringing Fantasy Alive for Children and Young Adults.* Linworth, 1999, 201pp.

About the Author

Annie Weissman has been working with libraries, schools, books and children for many years and in many capacities. She has been a high school teacher, children's librarian, elementary school librarian, faculty associate in library science at Arizona State University, principal, supervisor of student teachers at ASU West, public speaker and an author. A past recipient of The Progressive Library Media Award and the Excellence in Education Award, she is currently active in leadership positions in the Arizona Library Association. The author resides in Phoenix, Arizona.